AF268988

When THE PAIN REMAINS

When THE PAIN REMAINS

THE ROAD CALL LIFE

MARY BUCHANAN

Copyright © 2020 Mary Buchanan.

Haystack Creatives
8270 Woodland Center Blvd
Tampa, Florida 33614
www.haystackcreatives.com

ISBN: 978-1-953115-76-8 (sc)
ISBN: 978-1-953115-75-1 (e)

All rights reserved. No part of this book may be reproduced, stored, or transmitted by any means—whether auditory, graphic, mechanical, or electronic—without written permission of both publisher and author, except in the case of brief excerpts used in critical articles and reviews. Unauthorized reproduction of any part of this work is illegal and is punishable by law.

CONTENTS

In loving memory of my mother and brother
Louise Jones
Tommy James Maddox

Special thanks to my family for their support

INTRODUCTION

HAVE YOU EVER HEARD of a bean bus? Well, it was a one-way ticket to New York for my family when I was a young girl growing up in dire poverty in Alabama during the 1950s. While I felt quite isolated many times, thousands of families from Alabama, Florida and other Southern states caught rides to Upstate New York, chasing the chance to make enough money to feed and clothe their families.

As I begin my story in a hospital during the 1990's, it isn't the beginning of my story. It isn't even the end. No, my first reflection was the initiation for this project - the death of my mother. Though it is a cliché, life really is what happens while we're busy making plans. It wasn't until my dear momma's life was ending that I took the time to recall how we got to that small, sorrow-filled hospital room.

In the early summer of 1959, I was a young, black girl with four younger siblings, a mother who was barely putting food on the table for us and a step-father who had headed North months earlier, in search of a job and money. My mother and I had few resources to hold the family together, and what we had was drying up quickly. Then, like an angel, my mother's cousin drove into town with promises of a job and a better life, just for the summer, in Upstate New York picking beans for the season, living on a migrant camp. After a couple of days, our small family boarded a bean bus. Barefoot and hungry, we wished for little more than enough money to buy food and pay rent when we returned home at the end of the summer. However, there were different, bigger plans for us. Situations during that season made it impossible for us to return to Alabama. Little did we know our three-month visit to New York would last over three decades. In fact, my mother never returned to the South at all to live. Instead, she embarked on a life that included divorce, more children and entering the federal welfare system.

Being born to a sixteen year old who hid her baby in the woods because she feared her mother, I consider myself a diamond in the rough; every family has a diamond solitary. I was born for a purpose in my family. I believe God knew Mama needed me for what was ahead in her life. She gave birth to a son with a rare handicap when I was four years old. I was the one who would have to take care of him, the one who had to be strong for Mama during her weakness.

I wrote this book for healing and closure. I left behind all the sad memories in this book. I wanted to forget the fact my family was on welfare throughout my childhood. I wanted to forget the days of going without food. I wanted to forget the domestic abuse my mother endured. I needed the affirmation that I did not do so badly amidst all the adversity in my life as a child. I wanted to forget the pain that remains.

Letting go of the pain that remains in my life is due largely to my success of breaking the welfare cycle that was once a part of my existence Today, I am a better woman because of the hardship I endured. This is a story filled with sadness. It is with sincere hope that all who read this book will realize there is no greater love than the love of family.

CHAPTER 1

WHEN THE PAIN REMAINS PART 1

Berkshire Medical Center, Pittsfield, Massachusetts
March 29, 1993

I STOOD AT MY mother's bedside watching her motionless body, knowing her final breath was near. By the time I arrived at the Berkshire Medical Center in Pittsfield Massachusetts, Mama, had gone into a semi-coma. My state of mind very fragile, and I felt this would be my first and last time entering the doors of this hospital. I hastily hurried to her room, after getting off the elevator. Upon entering the dimly lit room with an overhead light above her bed, I glimpsed Mama, waiting to die, so helpless with fluids slowly dripping from the intravenous tubes into veins in her arm.

I tiptoed across the room, as if not to awake her, oblivious to any other surrounding. As I approached her bedside, I whispered to her that I was there. She knew and briefly opened her eyes. She never responded with words, just moved her fingers. It was as if she wanted to talk, but unable. In her hospital bed, as she remained so motionless, I wondered to myself if she made peace with God.

I touched her cheeks. They were so cold, and tears came streaming down my face. I did not want to see her the way she was, not talking or smiling.

I spent the previous weekend with her, leaving her Sunday going back home to Upstate New York. I had convinced my sister Sarah to take her to emergency room on Monday, March 22. Perhaps she would not have been in this state, if she had stayed home with her family. She had slipped into semi coma before I had a chance to have one last conversation.

I spoke with her the day she was admitted into the hospital, telling her I would call each day to check on her. I spoke to her each day through Thursday. She sounded good on the phone, but when I called Friday, she did not know whom she was talking to, and sounded confused. I kept repeating, "I'm coming to see you on next Saturday," which would have been April 4. The last words I heard her speak were "OK, bye."

I received a call Monday, March 29 from Sarah, telling me I needed to rush to Massachusetts, Mama was in a semi-coma, and I needed to be there. Sarah was so afraid and did not want to be alone at the hospital with Mama; she wanted the rest of the family at her side. My younger sister had seen Mama suffer so much during the months of taking care of her, and the reality of what would soon happen took a toll on her. I had planned to leave upstate New York to go see Mama in Pittsfield on the following Saturday, but instead I left immediately. I could not wait another day to see Mama.

She was almost to the end. I knew the time was coming for her departure, but I was not ready. I hoped for some type of miracle.

When Sarah took Mama to the hospital and she was admitted, her cancer was in the final stage. The previous October the doctors had given her six months to live. It had been six months exactly, since Mama's cancer was diagnosed. Now, as I stood at her bedside, I could not accept her leaving us.

———

Throughout the years, I had always been there for her and with her. We had only each other, when the rest of the children were too young to understand, what we were going through. We survived a move from Alabama to Upstate New York on a migrant bean bus, living in a migrant labor camp. Even though Mama would take her final breathe in another state, a place away from home, Upstate New York was the place she loved for so many years. Upstate New York had been our home for thirty-five years.

We lived through a lot of trials and tribulations in New York.

———

Mama, complained for some time about not feeling well. I was accustomed to her complaints; therefore, I never took her seriously. However, I did notice her strength decreased and she was not able to do the things she used to do. She loved to cook big dinners on Sundays and holidays, but she started having trouble standing to prepare meals.

A diabetic who took insulin shots, my mother never told me she felt well, when I asked. As I stood at her bedside with a pain in my heart, I asked myself why it happened to her, and wondered how long she had cancer, and we were not aware of it.

After Mama complained more often about not feeling well, I began to rely, "Mama, you should see a doctor."

She never replied when I made that suggestion. She had never been in the hospital for any illness, just when having a baby. She did not like to go to the doctor, unless she was forced. After she would not go to the doctor, I suggested she should take a vacation for a while.

My sister Sarah, who is the third oldest daughter of my family, and my brother Tyrone, lived in Massachusetts. Mama also had a sister in Massachusetts. Mama enjoyed being with Sarah and her children. Sarah had four daughters, who loved their grandma dearly. I called and told Sarah that Mama needed to get away for a while. I explained that something was going on with Mama. Within a few days, Sarah drove from Massachusetts to New York to pick up Mama. Mama was to spend a few weeks with Sarah, but as it turned out, she stayed in Massachusetts for almost a month. This was her first time away from home for so long. Sarah called to tell me that Mama was still not herself, and she complained of stomach pains frequently. Sarah wanted to take her to a doctor, but Mama refused to go. Sarah bought over-the-counter pain medication from the pharmacy for her, hoping those would solve the problem.

Mama turned 60 while she was in Massachusetts. Sarah, and her children threw a party to celebrate her birthday; it had been many years since she had any type of celebration in her life. Mama declared at her birthday party that it "will be her last birthday," but no one took her seriously.

I did not feel good when I heard about Mama's attitude. It seemed there would soon be changes in our life, But, I could not imagine life without her. We had been through a lot as a family.

Mama asked me to come to Massachusetts to pick her up after about a month with Sarah. She wanted to come home. At first, I did not want to drive to Massachusetts to pick her up, because we'd just had the first snow fall for the season and I was afraid of driving such a long distance. It was only two hours away, but with the snow it seemed a lot longer. As I contemplated, I knew I had to get her back home. If she was seriously ill and something happened to her in Massachusetts, I would never forgive myself.

I started out early on a Sunday morning to get Mama. She was already packed and sitting by the window, waiting for me, in a hurry to leave Massachusetts and get back to her own home. We left immediately after I arrived, which I did not mind. I did not trust the weather and wanted to get back to New York.

Mama did not say much on the drive home, and that worried me. I drove to her apartment and could see the happiness on her face as I stopped to let her out of the car. It felt good to see how happy she was to get back home. I knew I made the right decision and it was worth driving in the bad weather.

"Mama," I said, "do you need anything before I leave?"

"I will be fine. I'm just glad to be home," she replied.

"I'll call and check on you from time to time throughout the week," I said.

When I got back to my apartment, I called her, just to hear her voice again. I still did not like the feeling I had about Mama.

You see, Mama was the most important person to me. We had been through thick and thin together.

The next day was a workday for me; I began calling Mama around noon to check on her. There was no answer. At first, I figured she was doing something and did not hear the phone. I called every hour, on the hour, but never got an answer. By the end of the day, I felt very uneasy. It was not like her to be away from home, especially all day. Mama was never one who would go out often; she did not like shopping or anything that took her out of the house.

Later in life, I learned Mama had a phobia, one that had been with her for many years, agoraphobia. I was amazed to learn there was a name for her fear of leaving the house; many people share that fear. I had done everything for her, beginning at a very young age; the earliest I can remember was five years old. I had to do everything for Mama when I became big enough to take on the responsibility of helping take care of my siblings. Mama did not have to do any shopping. I did all the shopping for her, whether it was for food or clothing and shoes; I was there to do the things she needed done. Somewhere in her life, she lost interest in everything, but she still had dreams of one day owning her own home and car.

The worrying got the best of me. Then it dawned on me, maybe I should call the hospital emergency to see if she was there. I telephoned the hospital she would most likely visit. When the receptionist answered the phone, I ask if she had a Mrs. Jones as a patient in the emergency room. The receptionist replied she was typing up paperwork for Mrs. Jones. The receptionist explained that the emergency room doctor wanted to admit her into the hospital.

I immediately left work and went straight to the emergency room. I found a nurse and told her I was looking for my mama. She took me to the observation room Mama was in and proceeded to tell me Mama had come by taxi cab and an emergency room doctor wanted to run some tests.

My mama would never go anywhere alone. I knew then something was seriously wrong. Mama sat on the side of the bed in the observation room.

"What's the matter?"

"I'm sick," she responded. Mama was never lost for words. So, with such a short answer, I knew she was very sick.

The doctor came into her room, while I was there, and told me he was very concerned about her condition. Mama had jaundice. Her fingernails and eyes were yellow. The doctor explained he admitted her into the hospital because of diarrhea and fecal incontinence, things she never mentioned to me before. Her complaint to the doctor was she experienced four to six bowel movements a day, accompanied by abdominal cramps; she had no control of her bowel.

"Do you smoke, Mrs. Jones?"

"No, I do not smoke," Mama replied.

"Tell him the truth. You know you smoke," I prodded Mama.

Years of smoking could not have been good for her. I began to wonder if perhaps smoking had something to do with her illness.

Finally, Mama said to the doctor, "I do smoke a little bit."

Mama smoked for as long as I could remember. As a young girl, I walked in the snow to get cigarettes for her. She smoked a pack a day.

Mama had lost five to ten pounds. She always needed to lose weight, because she was an insulin-dependent diabetic. She never ate much, but she ate the wrong types of food. Being from the South, she loved salt pork, collard greens, fried chicken, buttermilk and cornbread. She was very overweight.

The next few days in the hospital, Mama had to undergo different tests – CT scan and ultra sound, along with many other tests. She never complained. She knew she was very ill. One test of the abdomen showed dilated bile ducts, slight prominence of the head of her pancreas, and a possible mass. An electrocardiogram and surgical consult with several doctors was scheduled. The doctor decided to do another CT of the pancreas. The plan was to take her to the operating room and do an exploratory laparotomy and possibly a palliative procedure.

I called Sarah to come and be with Mama during all the tests and procedures. I worked during the day and could not take the time off. My sister came to be with Mama. Sarah promised to call me to let me know what they found once a biopsy was completed.

Please, I pleaded with God, *do not let it be cancer.*

A biopsy of the head of the pancreas revealed adenocarcinoma of the pancreas. Sarah called me with the bad news. I hung up the phone and began to cry. I became very angry with God.

How could you let my mother get cancer?

"After all the suffering she had been through, raising eight children alone, not having anything good out of life, except her children". I screamed at God, How could you, God! How could you do this to her?

My heart ached so much, I felt betrayed by God, even though He had taken care of us many times. Even when there was not enough food to eat, He gave me ideas how to feed my family. I asked people for work cleaning their houses and ironing clothes during the winter months. Of course, during the spring, I picked strawberry, and the summer months I picked snap beans, until I became old enough to get a real job.

Why had God let Mama down now? This was the one time I could not do anything to help her. I could not change the situation. I felt alone, but it only lasted for a few moments.

I could not fall apart. Mama needed me. The rest of the family needed me. I was always there for them. I knew I had to snap out of my anger and make plans for Mama. Little did I know at the time, God had made all the plans for me and he was always there by my side, even in my time of anger.

After getting the news from my sister, I left work and went to the hospital. As I drove, I got angrier and angrier with God. I promised myself that when I became an adult and got a job, I would give Mama the things she desired and deserved, but it did not turn out that way. Life was not fair to her. I tried to do my best to help her. With the two of us, we survived life's hardship for many years, and I would tell myself, beginning as a young child, that life would get better. I was too young to know that life is not always as we planned.

My brothers and sisters did not depend on God as I had done all my life. They would not understand why I was so angry.

Dr. Martin, a cancer specialist, was assigned to care for Mama. He was a young doctor, who had already completed many surgeries for Mama's type of cancer. He explained to Mama everything he wanted to do. He wanted to perform surgery immediately. Mama asked Dr. Martin to explain the procedure to me.

So, the doctor requested an appointment with me. He explained what he wanted to do. I did not know exactly what he was talking about; all I remembered was the surgeon saying there was no guarantee the surgery would be successful. The procedure he wanted to do was called the Whipple surgery. As Dr. Martin talked about the procedure, I could sense the eagerness in his voice. This was the type of surgery he enjoyed performing. I was reluctant about her having surgery, because I knew she would never be the same. But, I was afraid if she did not have surgery and there was a chance she could get better and I had talked her out of it, I would not be able to forgive myself.

I could tell she really believed in the doctor and felt surgery would be the best for her. Just three weeks before her visit with Sarah in Massachusetts, she had laser surgery for diabetic retinopathy on her eyes. Up to this point in her life, it was her only surgery. After talking with my siblings, we decided to go along with the surgery. Mama had to endure many tests and procedures before the major surgery. She seemed to be feeling better while she awaited surgery. The night before surgery, she managed to get out of bed. We laughed and talked. She told me she had a dream about a roast beef sandwich. I brought her that sandwich to the hospital, even though she could not eat it.

On the day of Mama's surgery, all of her children, except my brothers Thomas and Rod, were at the hospital. It was hard for my brother in California to come home at the time and my younger brother Rod did not like hospitals. We waited together to hear from the doctor after her surgery. We waited for hours; finally, I saw the doctor approach us. I could tell something went wrong. The look on Dr. Martin's face was that of sadness. He explained to us about a tumor that covered two-thirds of Mama's pancreas. The doctor decided not to perform the Whipple, because of the extensive nature of the disease in the pancreas. He said doctors could do nothing more than make her comfortable. Dr. Martin removed her gall bladder, along with part of the common bile duct; he also put a temporary drain in her abdomen.

The doctor confided in us children that Mama had about six months to live.

"Dr. Martin," I said, "What caused Mama's pancreas cancer?"

"Just a case of bad luck," he replied.

Mama's luck had never been good, and now, it seemed to me, her bad luck would follow her to death.

———

As I stood at her bedside, watching and hoping for any type of movement, I realized it ended an era. My mind drifted back to the day my family left Alabama on a migrant bus, going to Upstate New York to pick beans for a season. Upstate New York should have been the place for Mama's final hours, because of our love for the place we called home for thirty-five years. I found my value in life as I grew up there. I learned to be strong, work hard and be the best person I could be. Leaving Alabama offered a chance for a better life, so I believed, even though it was to be four months, but instead ended up being thirty- five years.

I do not know why, but my life began to flash back. Seeing Mama lying there I thought back farther and farther to the beginning of our journey to New York. I began to remember the life in Alabama, and then in New York. I'd never thought about my life throughout the years since leaving Alabama. No one ever asked me how my family got to New York. It was like my past life escaped my memory all those years, but with Mama dying, it all came back to me. I became that eleven-year-old girl again as my mind drifted back to the beginning of our journey to, Upstate New York on a "bean bus."

CHAPTER 2

CAMP HILL, ALABAMA

June 11, 1959

IT ALL BEGAN ONE hot, summer day, when Cousin Betsy stopped by to visit with Mama. She came through Alabama on her way to Florida. Mama and Cousin Betsy were second cousins on my mother's maternal side of the family. They were very close in their younger years, had grown up together, gone to the same school and shared secrets as teenagers, so Mama told me. Her cousin left Alabama some years earlier. Betsy's mother and father were still there. She came home during the summer to visit her mother and father, but Mama never got a chance to see her. Betsy always left in a hurry. She did not like to stay around long, but this time she visited Mama.

I could tell Mama and her cousin had not seen each other for many years, by the way they hugged each other. Cousin Betsy told Mama how good she looked. Mama was a pretty lady. Her hair was short; she was a head taller than Cousin Betsy. Mama had a smooth pecan complexion, with dimples in her cheeks when she smiled. Her waistline was very tiny. She had big hips and big, pretty legs. I used to hear the men say she was built like, "a Coke Cola bottle."

I heard Mama talk about her cousin many times, about all the fun they had growing up together in the country. I felt like I knew her before she stepped in the door.

She was the most beautiful woman I had ever seen, with black, silky hair that seemed to glow with sheen. I wanted to touch her pretty hair. She was not very tall, just the right size for her height. Her skin was like a bronze doll. She had a gold tooth on the side of her mouth, and when she smiled, her eyes twinkled. She gave my three brothers, my baby sister and me a big hug.

My little sister Diann was only three years old; my brother Tyrone was four, Thomas was five, Tommy was seven and I was eleven. I was called by my middle name, Clara, but to my brothers and sister I was "gull," the name Tommy gave me when he first started to talk. He could not say Clara, so he just called me gull. Gull is a southern term for girl.

After Cousin Betsy finished hugging each of us, she and Mama talked about old times. I fell in love with Cousin Betsy right away; it was nice to get a hug. I never got hugs from other family members, not even from Mama, as far as I could remember. Cousin Betsy's mother told her Mama wanted to see her next time she came home, so she decided to visit. She said she had stopped in Alabama, because she and her boyfriend, Joe, were on their way to Florida to get a busload of migrant farm workers to pick beans.

Joe was a migrant worker crew leader. They came south from Upstate New York to get workers in Florida to take back North to pick beans for the season. It was Joe's job, as a crew leader, to get a busload of workers every June from Florida and other parts of the South, to take back to Upstate New York for work. After the season finished in October, he returned them back south.

Joe had a brand-new, gray car with a red strip across the doors, the biggest car I had ever seen. I thought to myself, *they must be rich.* Joe was a big man with a mustache and large, white teeth in the front of his mouth; he had a very dark complexion. He did not smile very much, or talk a lot neither. Joe did not seem to be a friendly person and he didn't look that good. I could not see what Cousin Betsy saw in him. She was so pretty and he was so ugly, but I could tell they were in love, by the way they held hands as they sat down. He just sat there while Cousin Betsy did all the talking.

It was good to have somebody come to our house; no one ever came to our house to see us, except Silas and Earlene. Mama said Silas was just her friend, but I knew he was her boyfriend. He came by our house mostly at night.

One of Mama's six sisters lived on the same long dirt road as we did, one lived in town. Two more lived in other parts of Alabama. One lived in Georgia and the last lived in Massachusetts. None came to our house. Two of them were a lot older than Mama. We did not see them often, but when they did visit, they all met on Sundays at the house they grew up in, where Aunt Katherine lived. We would always go to Aunt Katherine's house. Mama was close to her six sisters and she enjoyed when they all got together, but Katherine was the matriarch of the family. Other than her family, Mama did not like crowds. She was never away from home. Even though she never travelled, she loved to have visitors.

It was so good to have somebody from New York come to our house and that made me so happy. I never knew anybody from New York, but I used to hear Mama and her sisters talk about New York, how some girls left the South going to New York to work for rich people. Most of them got jobs taking care of children for rich folks. I was so excited, because I dreamed of going to New York when I grew up. To have someone come by our house from New York was more than I could take. I believed New York was a different world, one big city with bright lights everywhere and many people.

The only places I ever heard about were Alabama, California and New York. I did not know there were other places on earth. California was where all the movie stars lived and New York was the place everybody wanted to go for a job.

I heard Cousin Betsy telling Mama about Upstate New York, how she should come back with them to pick snap beans for the season. Mama told her Papa left for Pittsburgh, Pennsylvania, to look for work, and if he found a job, he would send for us. Papa would always leave us and not come back for months, but this time he was gone much longer.

I did not think he was ever going to send for us. Mama only had one letter from him, which somebody wrote for him.

Papa could not read or write. His letter was filled with promises — how he was going to buy us new clothes and shoes. He said he would send money home for food, once he found a job. Mama wanted him to come and help her with the three boys.

———

Papa was not my biological father. I was four years old and Mama was 20 when Mama married him; I was born when she was sixteen, in Camp Hill, Alabama. My maternal grandmother took care of me from the time I was born until I was four years old. Mama lived at home with her parents before she married Papa. After they had gotten married, they moved to a farm in Lochapolka, Alabama, They left me behind to stay with Grandma; I was old enough to know that I did not care, because I loved my Grandma and I wanted to stay with her. I finally had to go live with them when Grandma took sick and never got well. She died from diabetes. I was still four years old when she died.

I had to go live with Mama and her new husband before they were ready for me. They were still newlyweds. Mama packed me up and took me to live with her and her husband, after Grandma's funeral. I cried a lot for my Grandma and had to get used to living with Mama and Papa. Mama's father was a quiet little man, never said a word. He died six months after Grandma, from diabetes, too.

Mama was going to have a baby, so that took my mind off Grandma a little bit. The first week I was with Mama, she took me to the clinic to get my vaccination shots; she also had a doctor's appointment that day. It was raining just a little, and we had to cross a creek to get to the clinic. Mama said when it rained hard the creek rose and nobody could cross it. It started to rain very hard while we were at the clinic.

On the way back home, Mama noticed the creek had raised a lot, but she could not tell how much. She was scared to step into the water, because she did not know how high the water was, but we had to get home. Mama tightly held my hand and decided to step into the water. As soon as we started into the water, we were swept downstream by the swift current. Mama held my hand as the water took us downstream, both of us screaming. Mama noticed a tree branch leaning in the creek. With her free hand, Mama caught the branch and pulled us out of the creek.

I had a new, yellow dress with a red flower on it. How I liked that dress! It was the only new dress I remember. As we got out of the water, I looked down at my dress, the red flower had faded into my yellow dress and the dress was ruined. I remember being very sad about that dress. I had my first experience of fear living with Mama.

I was so lonesome living on the farm. I sat on the porch and watched the men cut down trees and load wood on a truck. Sometimes, the driver of the truck told me he would bring me some oranges from town. He had to go unload the truck, he said to me. I sat on the porch all day, looking for his truck. He always kept his promise, bringing me oranges. Maybe it was not a whole day, but it felt like it to me. Getting the oranges was the one thing that made me happy.

I had only been with Mama a short while before my oldest brother was born. I was nearly five years old. Tommy was sickly and had to have special care. He was born with a rare illness and stayed in the hospital many times. The nearest hospital for Tommy's illness was in Birmingham, Alabama, a hundred miles away. Mama took the Greyhound bus with Tommy; I do not remember Papa ever going with her.

The day Tommy was born; a woman came to our house with a little black suitcase. She told me she had a baby in her case, and, soon. I would have a brother or sister. Papa told me I had to stay outside and play in the yard while the woman took care of Mama. I heard Mama screaming and I wanted to peek, but I was scared. Papa stayed in the house while the woman with the black suitcase was in the room with Mama. After a while, Papa ran out of the house with the baby wrapped in a blanket and told me to get into the car, Mama and the woman were close behind. Once Mama got into the car, Papa gave her the baby. I did not understand what was happening; I just got in the car.

Papa had an old, beat-up, black Studebaker. I did not know if the baby was a boy or girl at that point. When we got to the hospital in Tuskegee, Alabama, there were doctors and nurses running everywhere. They swept the baby into the operating room. While the doctors operated, Mama told me I had a baby brother, but he was very sick. I asks Mama about the lady with the little, black suitcase; she explained she was a midwife. I did not know what she meant by midwife or when she said my brother was sick.

We waited for many hours before the doctor came to get Mama. I just sat still, and was scared as she left with the doctor. When Mama came back to me, she told me we had to leave my baby brother in the hospital.

Tommy was named after Papa. He stayed in the hospital two weeks. When he came home, he had what looked like a sore on his stomach. Mama told me it was actually his intestines. She said the doctors cut him in the middle of his stomach to bring out his large and small intestines so he could get rid of waste from his body. Also, there wasn't an opening on his backside for him to pass his bile. The only other way for him to pass his bile was from his mouth. That is why he had to have an operation soon after he was born. I did not understand, until I was older, that Tommy was born without an anus.

I did not care my brother was different. I wanted to help Mama take care of him. I wanted to change his diapers the first day he came home from the hospital. At first, she would not let me. Mama put a small cloth over his stomach and then, put his diaper on. When I became five years old, I changed his diaper and Mama helped me, being careful not to hurt the sore on his stomach. I wanted to change him every chance I got. Little did I know it would be my job for years to come. When he was too large for regular diapers, I pinned the diaper around his stomach like a waistband. It got harder and harder for me to keep him clean as he grew older and taller, and I began to dislike changing him.

I washed the few diapers Tommy had by hand in a pail each day. I spent most of my time taking care of him and washing his diapers by hand, Oh! How I hated it. I took care of him until he was old enough to take care of himself. Though it was only until he was seven or eight years old, it seemed like forever before he was old enough to care of himself.

———

Cousin Betsy kept right on talking about how good things would be up North. I could tell Mama was thinking when she told Cousin Betsy she did not have any money, and with five children it would be too hard. Cousin Betsy said Mama did not need any money; Joe would take care of everything. They told Mama everyone would start picking beans right away, once the bus got to New York. We would stay in the migrant labor camp. It was never said how much money she would make in New York, if she decided to go, but whatever it was, it was more than we had.

Mama said she would think about going to New York and asked them to stop by on their way back from Florida. Joe said it would take him three days to get the workers he needed before they came back through Alabama. He explained he had a bus and a driver, once he got to Florida. They promised Mama they would save seats for us, just in case. To me it was a chance for Mama to work and make some money for us, so I had to do whatever I could to get her to go to New York.

———

We lived in the country. It was so dark at night, as I stared toward town at night, I could see the lights peeking over the trees far, far away. My mind drifted away to a place I dreamed of going, a place where there would be no more dark roads at night. The darkness of the night did not keep grownups from going to visit friends and family. The stars in the sky led the way down the old, dark, dirt roads at night. I wanted to go where there was streetlights, and New York was that place.

The house we lived in was an old, white house that used to be a store years ago, setting on stacks of large stones alongside a dirt road. The store moved to a new store across the road from us. It had a light in the front yard, but when they closed at night, everything was dark. At night, the lights shined through the windows of the old houses on the dirt road that had electricity. Not every house had electricity. The storefront house we lived in had electrical wires to the house. Sometime we had lights, but most of the time the men would come and turn our lights off. We did not have any money to pay for power. The only light we had when our electric lights were turn off was a Kerosene Lamp, and there were times, we did not have any kerosene for the lamp, we would just sit in the dark. During the winter months, the fireplace was our light at night.

The only time I saw streetlights up close was when I went to Aunt Frankie's house in town. Sometimes, Mama let me spend the night with Aunt Frankie's kids. I never wanted to come home after spending the night with them; I did not want to come back to the dark country.

It just had to be better in New York! It had to be better. This was what I had been dreaming about, leaving the country for the city. I had to make Mama see how good it would be, if we left on the migrant bus going to New York.

I was scared of the dark, mostly because the older folks told ghost stories about animals coming out of the graves in the cemetery. They talked about seeing ghosts walking at night and seeing someone from our family who had died years ago, looking through the windows. When I went to bed, I was too scared to sleep with my head uncovered. I pulled the quilt over my head, just leaving my nose out to breathe. I did not want to see a ghost.

My great-aunt Rosa had taken sick and died only a few months before Cousin Betsy stopped by our house that June morning, and Aunt Rosa lived in the house close to ours. It was a custom to bring the body of the dead person home, for the last time, the night before the funeral. The undertaker would set up the casket in the family home of the dead person, the night before the funeral. Aunt Rosa's body was home the night before her funeral. The casket was placed in the hallway, for people to come by to visit with the family and see her body. I will never forget the fear of seeing Aunt Rosa's body in her house, lying in that casket. I can remember the undertaker touching my arm saying, "little girl go outside and bring some wood in for the fireplace." I screamed so loud, I could have woken the dead.

I cried as I went outside to get the wood. The feel of the undertaker hands on my arm was as if Aunt Rosa herself has touched me. I was scared; I did not want him touching me. I heard the older folks talk about seeing Aunt Rosa looking through the window at night. She had only died in April and Betsy came down in June. I heard my uncle Douglas, Aunt Rosa's husband, say she came through the window, one night and got in the bed with him, he claimed she was cold. Just to hear him say that made me scared. Not one night passed that I did not think about all the ghosts.

Every month, when there was a full moon, I felt a little at ease. The moon shined and lit up the whole outside. I looked forward to the full moon. It was the only time I went outside at night, I looked up at the full moon, twirling around with outstretch arms singing to it, "I see the moon. The moon sees me. Please, Mr. Moon, don't tell it on me." It was so beautiful glowing at night, if only it lasted forever.

I could not wait to grow up, so I could leave the South. Now, we had a chance to leave the South and Mama acted as if she did not want to leave. I had to make her see that we had to go up North.

There were two rooms in our house, a kitchen and one large room for our bedroom and front room. The only heat was the fireplace in the winter; I carried wood, sometime cutting down small trees for firewood. Every morning, I woke for school and made a fire in the fireplace, got dressed and waited for the school bus while Mama remained in bed.

I never had anything to eat before leaving for school in the morning, but I received free lunches. I wanted to go to school; I look forward to lunch every day. Sometimes, we ate collard greens, fried chicken and cornbread, which was a favorite.

I was there for Mama. I babysat for her when she went to work cleaning house, washing and ironing for white folks. I cooked for the rest of the children. I chopped wood for cooking, as well as the fireplace. I learned to cook on the old, black, wooden stove in the kitchen, but all I ever cooked was biscuits and rice for my brothers and sister. My biscuits never turn out right, always brown on the outside and raw dough on the inside. My brothers cried, because they did not want to eat the biscuits I made for them. They called my biscuits dough bread, but I made them eat anyway.

I was only eleven years old, but sometimes I was more like their mother, rather than their big sister. I learned to cut wood when I was eight years old. I had been cutting wood more since Papa left.

Even though our house was very old, it was all we had. Every summer, snakes came from under the house and Mama killed them with a hoe. My brothers did not know enough to be scared of the snakes, so some times they came close to getting bit, but I was scared of snakes, and I knew enough to get away from them.

I did not like living in that house. There had to be something better than where we lived, and I hoped we would find a good place to live, so with a chance to go to New York, I pleaded and cried for Mama to take us there.

After crying and pleading for a whole day, Mama got tired of me crying, and at last said we would go. I felt happy inside. I had the biggest smile frozen on my face. My brothers and little sister were happy, too, even though they did not understand. I believed deep down inside

Mama knew Papa would not come home soon and she could not take care of us cleaning house, and the forty-four dollars a month she got from welfare. By the time we were set to return in October, maybe Papa would come home to take care of the family.

We only had two days to see the rest of the family and say good-bye before we left. We saw Mama sister Katherine, Aunt Shoke and Grandma Lillie before we left. Grandma Lillie was Mama's grandma; she lived with her daughter Shoke, down the road from us. We called Grandma Lillie Granny, She was in her eighties. Saying goodbye to her and her daughter was so hard. Granny cried when Mama told her we were heading to the North. I loved Granny and knew I would miss her. I hated to see her cry, but we had to go to New York. I did not know, at that time, I would never see Granny or her daughter again.

Mama had sisters who lived not far from us, we wanted to say goodbye to them, but we only had a chance to see one of her six sisters before we left. Mama was very close to Katherine, my favorite aunt. Katherine was the only one we saw before we left. When Mama told Katherine

she was going to New York and that we would be back in October, Katherine asks Mama if she knew what she was doing leaving with five children. Mama explained she was going to New York for her children. Katherine knew Papa was in Pittsburgh and she knew how hard it had been for us. After giving us her blessing, she told Mama to hurry back.

Mama and I started packing our few pieces of clothes. There were not many clothes at all to pack, and we did not have any shoes to wear or pack. Mama had a beat up pair of house slippers, a pair of high heels. She wore her house slippers on the bus to New York. The rest of us traveled barefooted.

Mama had fifteen cents to her name, the only money we took to New York. She never had much money, just what Mrs. Francis paid her for cleaning her house. We did get forty-four dollars a month from welfare, but there was nothing left after rent and a few groceries. Mrs. Francis paid her two dollars a day and Mama bought cigarettes with part of that.

Mama could not tell Cousin Betsy she only had fifteen cents. It was better to tell them she had nothing.

Mama wanted to buy something for us to eat on the bus. She tried to borrow some money from Katherine, but Katherine said she did not have any money, so we had no choice but to believe Joe when he said that he would take care of everything on the way to New York.

Even though she was afraid of leaving Alabama, once Mama made up her mind we were leaving, she would have left Alabama, even if Joe had not said he would take care of everything. She had to be tired of waiting for Papa; there was no food in the house, except rice.

The bus from Florida came early Friday morning. Joe and Cousin Betsy stopped by the house. They were glad she decided to go back with them. Joe took Cousin Betsy back to her mother and father's house, where the bus was parked, and then Joe came back to pick us up, to take us to the bus. I could not stop smiling as Mama and all five of us children piled into Joe's car.

When we got to the bus, there were people standing around watching and waiting for the bus to leave. It seemed everyone in the country knew a busload of people had stopped at Cousin Betsy's parents' house, and that the bus was headed to New York. Almost everyone was from Florida, all going to pick beans. I felt so good to be around all the peoples going north. Picking beans sounded like a real good job.

As I looked around, I saw Mama's friend Silas standing on the other side of the road looking at the bus. Silas was another reason I wanted to leave Alabama, because of what he did to Mama. He must have found out about us leaving from Katherine. He looked very sad, but I hated him for what he had done to my Mama. I knew I would never like him again. I did not want her to wave good-bye to him, but she did anyway.

———

Silas became a part of our family, especially after Papa had been gone for so long. Everybody in the country knew each other; Mama had known Silas for a long time. I liked him and he seemed to like all of Mama's children. He was easy to get along with, until a Sunday evening when something went wrong. Mama left me home to babysit the other kids, while she went to her friend Earlene's house with Silas, for a birthday dinner. Mama never left us alone, unless she was going to clean house for Mrs. Francis. I was eleven years old and she knew I could watch the other children.

Mama was not gone long before she came back with a scary look on her face. I asked why she came back home so soon, then I noticed her dress had cuts in the front. I started to cry, as she told me what happened. She said Silas cut up her dress and she was lucky he did not cut her. Mama told me that when Silas got to Earlene's house he was a different person. As they were sitting next to each other at Earlene's house, without warning, he starts cutting the front of her dress.

Mama left home in the only good dress she had, a baby blue and pink plaid dress. She looked very pretty when she left for Earlene's house. Mama said she did not know Silas at all; all he wanted to do was fight with her. I was afraid Silas would come to our house to start with her again. No one ever knew the fear I felt inside that day; I was so afraid, my stomach began to ache.

The evening was still early, when Mama came home. I sat waiting for Silas to come to our house. As it got dark, and Silas had not come to our house, I just knew he would come at night. I continued to feel sick on the stomach, so scared for Mama. My brothers and little sister did not know what happened between Silas and Mama. As the night came, Mama and my baby sister sat on one bed, while my brothers and I sat on the other bed. When we heard footsteps on the front porch, I started crying because I knew it was Silas. The other children cried, too. Mama jumped from the bed and ran to make sure the doors were locked.

There were two front doors to our house – one door on each side of the front porch, but no back door. The porch was as long as the house, one door leading into the kitchen and the other one into the front room. By the time Mama checked the doors, we heard Silas yelling on the porch and beating on the door facing the front room. When he found that door locked, he went to the other door, still yelling and beating on the door. Silas realized the doors were locked, he went to the only window and that was facing the front porch, next to the door of the bedroom and front room. In a hurry, Mama made sure the doors were lock, but she forgot about the window. The window was up a little. Silas started raising the window up from the outside, enough for him to climb into the house.

Mama got all of us children together as Silas put his last leg in the window. Mama unlocked the door in the kitchen and we ran outside the house and waited near the road, while he was left in the house. Mama grabbed an old pistol that belonged to Papa before running out of the house with us. She did not know if the pistol was any good or not. It was old and rusty, but she told Silas she had a gun and would shoot him if he came near us. It was dark outside and he did not know the gun was old and rusty. It seemed like he had been drinking, but he was not that drunk. Silas was afraid to come out of the house.

We waited outside near the road, facing the house for a long time. Silas was quiet inside the house. There was no way Mama would take us back into the house while he was still in there. I stopped crying, because I felt safe while Mama had a gun.

Silas came to the door after a long while and said he wanted to leave, that he was not going to bother Mama; all he wanted to do was to leave and go home. He came out one door and we went back in the house through the other door. Mama locked both doors.

I will never forget that Sunday night, one of the worst nights of my life. Every night I was scare Silas would come back. I do not know how Mama felt inside, but I am sure she was afraid, too.

Monday came and passed, no Silas. Tuesday passed, no Silas. We did not see Silas until that Wednesday night. He knocked on the door. All of us had gone to bed. Mama and I were still awake. As soon as I heard Silas knocking on the door, I got up and sat on the side of the bed, scared for Mama. She got out of bed, begging him to go away. He claimed he just wanted to talk, and that he was sorry for what he had done to her.

I told Mama not to let him in, but she believed him when he said he was sorry. She opened the door to let him in, and went to lie back down in her bed. Silas set on the side of Mama's bed and they started to talk. I sat on the edge of the bed, because I was not happy about him being at our house. I had the same sick feeling I had that Sunday. I was afraid he was going to start with Mama again, but she told me to go back to bed, and Silas promised me he did not want to fight with Mama.

Silas did not look mad as I looked at him, so I went back to bed. I could hear Mama and Silas talking low, but I could not hear what they said.

I had just drifted off to sleep, when I heard Mama say to Silas in a loud voice, "what are you doing?"

I sat up to see what happened. The room was partly dark with the kerosene lamp turned down low. Mama looked at her upper arm and said, "You are cutting me."

She did not see the knife Silas had, but she felt him cutting her arm. As he talked to her while she was lying in bed, he had a knife and was cutting on her left arm. She felt the blood on the sheet. He put two long cuts in Mama's upper left arm, before she knew he was cutting her.

When I heard Mama say, "You are cutting me," I jumped out of bed and screamed. I screamed so hard and loud Silas just left out of the door. He never said a word. I felt as though I would stop breathing. Mama could not calm me down. She never let me know she was afraid. There was no one to hear my screams anyway. He did not have to leave if he did not want to, and just out of the goodness of God, he left. I was glad he did not hurt Mama more. Her cuts turned out to be not so deep. She did not need stitches.

Even if Mama needed stitches, there was no way to get to a doctor. The only doctor was in town, eight miles away. Silas did not have a car. He walked to our house. The closest person with a car was a few miles away. I do not know if my screaming scared Silas away, but I knew I would never like him again.

All this happened just a few weeks before Cousin Betsy stopped by our house, telling Mama about New York.

Did God send Cousin Betsy by our house that day? I had been praying for help. I did not know what Silas wanted to do to Mama, all I knew was I would not have to worry about Silas hurting my Mama, at least for four months.

———

The bus was full, except for three seats; Mama had to hold my little sister. I shared my seat with one of my brothers, and my other two brothers shared a seat. We did not mind that it was crowded. I was just happy to leave Alabama. That Friday morning in June, after the bus took off, I was the happiest I had ever been in my life. Joe and Cousin Betsy rode in Joe's car, leading the way for the bus. Joe said it would take about three days to get to upstate New York, and we would stop to rest and eat.

As it turned out, the bus stopped a lot, because it kept breaking down. Joe and the bus driver repaired it. We had plenty of time to play outside while they were fixing the bus; we were the only children on the bus.

Everybody on the bus brought food with him or her. They had crackers and soda drinks. We did not have any food of our own to eat, but some people on the bus shared. When I was asked if I wanted something, I always said I did not. I think the reason they gave my brothers something to eat, was because my brothers kept staring at people while they were eating. Joe had food for us, once the bus stopped for rest, we ate. He was responsible for food, because he was the crew leader. The women, on a small charcoal grill at the rest areas, cooked hot dogs and hamburgers. There was water to drink with the meal; we only ate once a day. Mama did not eat at all; all she did was smoke her Pall Mall cigarettes she bought before we left.

I really felt that at last there would be happiness for my family. I was too young to think of what would be ahead for us.

Mama seemed to be at ease as the bus rode down the road, but deep down inside I knew she was not sure if she was doing the right thing. I promised her I would be the best babysitter I could be, while she picked beans. Being the oldest, it was my duty to look after the younger ones.

———

I was a blessing to Mama, because God knew she would need me to help her with the hard times in her life. I was born when she was sixteen years old. She did not get a chance to finish high school, dropping out in the eleventh grade. She knew I would do whatever she wanted me to do to help with my brothers and sister; after all, I was like a second mother to them. I always looked out for them. In New York, I would be even better helping Mama.

With Mama working, I thought I could get a new pair of shoes. I had not had a pair of shoes, since the ones my Aunt Katherine bought me for Christmas two years ago. They were white with a big, silver buckle on top. I never liked those shoes, and was glad the pair wore out. They did last me until school finished in May. I only wore shoes for school or church. I did not think there was anything wrong with going barefooted, but a pair of shoes would be nice. My feet had gotten bigger and hard on the bottom after going barefooted for so long. I could walk on rocks and not feel a thing.

I really wanted a new dress, too; it had been so long since I had a new dress. My cousin once told me that if I saw a pretty butterfly to catch it, and if I wanted a dress that looked just like the butterfly, I would have to bite the head of the butterfly off and make a wish, and then throw it behind my back, and then I would get a dress just like that butterfly. There were so many beautiful butterflies flying around. After trying what my cousin told me to do and never getting a new dress, maybe I would get a new dress in New York.

CHAPTER 3

REMEMBERING

DURING THE NIGHT, AS we traveled down the road, my mind wondered about what we left behind. There were no good memories left behind. I thought about the many times I had hurt in my life, the many times I was sad. There were many times I did not know what happiness was.

Happiness to me was going across the road to the store on a Sunday to watch television and drink a grape soda. Mr. Robert and his brother, Mr. Casey, owned the store; they also owned the storefront house we rented. There was a room in the back of the store with a television, which Mr. Robert and Mr. Casey would let children watch on Sundays. Only one family up the road owned a television, the only other television I got to watch. We went to their house to watch *Wagon Train* on Wednesday nights. I liked the news during the weekdays. I looked forward to the news. Huntley and Brinkley news came on in the evening and that is what I liked the most. As I stood in the front yard of our house, I could hear the news from the television at the store across the road.

I thought of the time Papa moved the family to Florida. He had a sister in Florida we could live with until he found a job, so he moved us from the farm in Alabama to Florida. His sister, Essie was a hairdresser; she fixed hair out of her home. She was nice to us and we stayed with her for a while. Her husband was away in the Army, so she was glad to have someone living with her.

Papa found a job not long after we move to Florida and things were going good for us. We surprised Aunt Katherine sometimes by going to Alabama to see her on the weekend. Whenever I saw Aunt Katherine and the house I use to live in, I realized how homesick I had been. Aunt Katherine had left her husband, and moved back with her son into the same house she had grown up in, to me that was still Grandma's house, even though she died. That was home, the only home I knew before moving with Mama and Papa, I felt happy living in that house, and I could feel Grandma's spirit there.

I missed my Aunt Katherine so much, until one weekend Mama and Papa drove me back to Alabama to live with her for a while. My Aunt Katherine loved me a lot; I could tell she did, even though she didn't give me hugs.

Mama had another baby, while we were living with Essie, so now she had three children. Mama had a baby boy; she named him Thomas. I had to go back to Florida to help her. Papa got a place for us to move after the baby was born. Eleven months later, she had another baby boy name Tyrone. Eleven months later, she had another baby, this time a baby girl name Diann. After Diann was born, Papa lost his job in Florida, and moved the family back to Alabama.

We stayed in Florida what seems to be a long time; it was long enough for Mama to have three more children. We did not have anywhere to live once we got back to Alabama, except with Aunt Katherine. Mama moved us in with her sister and Papa went off looking for work again. He went back to Florida without the family. All the while Papa was gone, Mama only heard from him once. He said he was going to buy us new clothes and shoes. He promised he would send money home for food, which we never got.

Aunt Katherine did her best to help us, but with six more people in her house, it was too much for her new husband to take. He was always getting mad with her about us living with them, even though it had been my grandma's house before he lived there, but he paid all the bills. Aunt Katherine did not work. Once in a while she picked cotton and took me with her.

Her husband, Eddie, worked on the railroad and he came home on the weekend, every two weeks. He and Mama always got along real good. She liked him a lot and he liked her, up until we moved in with them. After that, things changed. I guess it was too much for him to feed so many children. He made sure Aunt Katherine and her son from her first marriage had everything they needed. He was a real good father.

However, when he came home on the weekend, he would go out, get drunk and come back home to start a fight with Aunt Katherine. He told her he wanted us to move out of the house. I loved living with Aunt Katherine and my favorite cousin. Aunt Katherine always cooked good food. At first, she fed us when she cooked, but with her husband fussing all the time, she could not feed us when he was home. Mama cooked separate for us.

I wanted to eat what Aunt Katherine cooked. She always cooked good food like pork, beef and chicken. I could not understand why we had to eat separate. I felt like we did not belong to the family anymore. Aunt Katherine gave Mama a few dollars to buy a little food. Mama always cooked rice, salmon patties and biscuits.

I knew Aunt Katherine wanted us to eat together, but she did not want her husband to be angry, even though she was not afraid of him. Most of the time, when they fought, he ended up running from her. He made good money on the railroad; he was good to his family, if only Papa had been as good at taking care of his family.

Mama waited too long for Papa to come home; he had been gone for a long time. He was always going to find work. When he came home, he never had money. It seems to me God always took care of us, when we needed him the most. With Aunt Katherine's husband telling Mama she had to take her children and leave their house, it just so happen Mama had another sister who was married, she and her husband moved to Massachusetts. When she found out she was expecting a baby, she wanted the baby to be born in Alabama. Aunt Gloria husband's family owned a house no one lived in, and the house was available for any of their family who wanted to live there. Aunt Gloria wanted to live in the house until she had her baby and then go back to Massachusetts.

Her husband could not come down South with her, because he had to work. She did not want to live alone, so she asked Mama if she wanted to move in with her, to help while she was pregnant. Mama said she would move in, even though she knew it would only be for a short time. I was glad to live with Aunt Gloria. Christmas was coming and Mama didn't have money to buy me or my brothers and little sister anything. I knew Aunt Gloria would buy me something for Christmas, especially since I was the oldest. I was eight years old. As it turned out, Aunt Gloria bought me a plaid, suitcase record player. That Christmas morning was one of the happiest days of my life.

My cousin Will, Aunt Katherine's son, got a new bike for Christmas. He drove his bike to Aunt Gloria's house to show me. I was so excited about my record player and he was so excited about his bicycle. I wanted Aunt Katherine to see my record player, so Will said he would ride me on the back of his new bicycle to his house to show Aunt Katherine my record player. He put my record player on the handlebar of his bicycle and I sat on the back of his bicycle.

Will and I were happy as we started down the dirt road to his house. He drove as fast as he could. I held on to him, grinning. I did not know how to ride a bicycle yet. As we flew down a steep hill on the rocky, dirt road, I told him how good his bike rode, when all of sudden we hit a pile of rocks and the bicycle wrecked. Both of us fell off the bike. First, we dusted off our clothes. Then, I picked my record player up from the ground.

"Are you hurt?" Will asked.

I said no, but then he looked at me and said, "Your eye is bleeding!"

I did not know if I should start crying or not.

"Your eye is cut very bad!"

I raised my hand to touch my eye and felt a cut underneath the lower lid of my right eye, where a sharp rock cut me. We both decided

I should go back home, and he should go home. So I turned around to walk back home and he started down the road on his bicycle.

"Are you crying?" Will asked

I promised him I wasn't crying. As I got to the house, Mama was sweeping off the back porch. I had my hand over my eye.

"What happen to you"? Mama asked.

There was no blood. As I took my hand down from my eyes, she said, "Lord what happen?" I told her what had happen.

I went into the house, looked in a mirror and then I started to cry. The bottom lid of my eye was gapping wide open.

Mama walked up the road to a neighbor's house, to get a ride to take me into town to see the doctor. The doctor's office was closed, but there was a note on his door that said he was fishing at the creek down the hill from his office. We found the doctor on the creek fishing; he looked at my eye and said I needed stitches. We followed him back up the hill to his office.

The doctor began to sew my cut up right away. I received four stitches. Then, he put a patch over my eye. By the time we came back from the doctor, Aunt Katherine and Will were waiting for us. Will had gotten a bad whipping from Aunt Katherine. All the family felt sorry for me, but I felt special with the patch over my eye. I would never forget that Christmas. Little did I know at that time, the scar under my eye would be there for the rest of my life.

We stayed with Aunt Gloria less than a year. Aunt Gloria and her husband made up their mind that she should remain in Alabama for a while longer after she had her baby, so her father-in-law built them a small house on land he already owned. The house would be there if they ever wanted to move back South. It did not take long to build the new house. After the house was finish, she moved in with her baby and left us in her in-laws' house. We were able to stay in that house, just as long as none of the family wanted it for themselves.

When Aunt Gloria moved into her new house, she took the stove with her, so Mama did not have anything to cook on, so she used the fireplace. Mama cooked in the fireplace, placing a piece of tin over the hot wood. She cooked in the fireplace very good.

Eventually, one of the in-laws' family members wanted to move into the house, so we had to move out. Once again, we had nowhere to go. Aunt Katherine told Mama about the storefront house that was for rent, so Mama went to the welfare office for help. That's how we were able to live in our last home in Alabama. Katherine gave her two old beds and an old, black wood stove for cooking. We had a place of our own at last, but I was not happy. I wanted to live with one of my aunts, because they seem to have a better living than what Mama had. I hated the storefront house; I hated not having enough food. At least living with Aunt Gloria, we had good food to eat. Her mother-in-law sent freshly churned buttermilk and butter. Whenever she ate, she made sure we ate.

Many times, we ate cornbread and buttermilk for supper, but that was all right with me, as long as we had something to eat. Now, in our own house, we were lucky if we got fresh milk at all. After Momma paid the rent, there was very little money.

We lived in the storefront house a few months before Papa returned from Florida. Papa had been leaving, off and on, ever since he moved us back from Florida. He did not bring any money home and didn't have any new clothes for us. The only work he did when he came home was cut a little wood; he went hunting for rabbits when he felt like it. He stayed with us for a short time, before he decided to leave for Pittsburgh. Once again, he had family he could live with up North. He knew Mama needed help with Tommy, being that he was sickly and all, even though I was glad he was gone.

I loved Papa a lot, until I started to be afraid to be alone with him, but I did not think Papa loved me. When I was six years old, Papa tried to teach me to write my alphabet. The only problem, he could not read or write himself. I remember sitting at the table with him trying to learn how to write, and him hitting my hands, because I wrote with my left hand. He wanted me to write with my right hand. After hitting my hand so many times, I learn to write with my right hand. Being left-handed was a sign something was wrong with you, in Papa's mind. Mama never stopped him from hitting my hands; she just let him do it.

———

Mama had a job, cleaning house once a week for Mrs. Francis, an older white woman, Mama had been working for since she was a little girl. One morning, she left early while we were still in bed. Papa was home with us, while Mama went to work. Papa and my little sister were in the bed he and Mama slept in. Papa told me to get in the bed with him, where it would be warmer. I normally slept with my three brothers in the other bed. The house was very cold in the early morning during the winter months, until Papa started a fire in the fireplace. I was happy to get in their bed, because my baby sister slept with Mama and Papa and their bed was very warm. I would lie in Mama's spot. I got in the bed with Papa and my little sister. My little sister was always in the middle, but this day Papa told me to lie next to him. I did as he told me.

Papa started to feel on my chest, I was only nine years old. I just laid there, afraid to say anything, but when he told me to touch him in a place I knew was wrong, I said, "I don't want to do that."

I did not feel right touching him down there. He got mad at me and told me to get out of his bed, and I had better not tell. Papa was going hunting for rabbits and he knew I loved rabbit. He warned me that if I told Mama what happened, I would not get any rabbit.

Whenever he felt like it, he went hunting for rabbits for supper and Mama fried them up. Therefore, when he said not to tell, there was no way I was going to tell Mama and miss out on getting some fried rabbit. I never told Mama, but I did not feel the same about Papa anymore.

———

I did not want Papa to do to me what his brother Frank had done to me when I was only six years old. The memoir was still fresh in my mind when Mama decided to take us to New York. It happened when Frank was twenty-one years old, and married, but was not with his wife. Frank came to live with us when we lived in Lochapolka Alabama. Frank came to work with Papa on the farm; Papa was in charge of the farm and he needed some help, and at that time, the only person helping him was Mama.

Even though Mama had my brother Tommy, she still worked on the farm. I watched Tommy, while she went to the fields to help with the crops. She put a pot of black-eyed peas on the stove to cook for supper while she was in the field. I pulled a chair up to the stove and stood in the chair to stir the peas, so dinner would not burn.

Mama was glad to have Frank help out on the farm. We did not have a bed for Frank to sleep in, so he slept with me. I slept alone, until Frank came to the farm. Tommy slept with Mama and Papa,

At first, Frank would let me cuddle under him, and I like that a lot. As the time went by, every night when we went to bed, Frank would ask me to touch him in places I did not want to, but I did. He started to get on top of me. I thought it was wrong, but wasn't sure. He made me promise not to tell Mama. However, I began to tell Mama about being sore, so she checked me. She asked me if Frank messed with me, I told her no. She asked Frank anyway. He said he had never messed with me. That night, when I went to bed, Frank was angry with me. "Why you told your mama on me?" Frank demanded.

I promise him that I did not tell, so the same thing kept happening. Mama kept checking for signs that Frank was messing with me. One day, Mama called him to the side and told Frank to leave.

***

To have Papa try the same thing, I could not take, so I felt good having him away, regardless of the fact Mama needed him. She had me, I kept telling myself, and I would help her raise my brothers and sister.

Mama came from a big family, she was the seventh of ten children; there were seven girls and three boys, all of them afraid of their mother.

Mama said her mother was a very mean woman. I guess raising ten children; she had to be that way. Mama told me about her father. She said he was always sad because Grandma acted so mean to him. He was afraid of his wife as much as the children were. I remember Grandma Mary, even at four years old. I was special to her and I never knew why until I got older. I was named after her.

After Papa left for Pittsburgh, Mama continues to cleaned and washed for Mrs. Francis once a week. I watched the other kids while she worked. One day, Mrs. Francis asked Mama if it was all right for me to cut her grass for her. She asked Mama if I knew how to use a sling blade. Mama told her I never used a sling blade before, but Mrs. Francis offered to teach me.

As I left the house to walk to Mrs. Francis's house, Mama yelled to me, "You have to use the back door." Colored people could not use the front door. I never told her I knew I had to use the back door. Mrs. Francis had fussed at me already, the last time I went to her house to pick up something for Mama. I went to her front door, because I did not know any better and she told me, "little girl, never use the front door again, you go around to the back door."

Mrs. Francis showed me how to use a sling blade. It was hard trying to cut the grass with the sling blade, but I did not mind, because I wanted to make some money to help my family with food. I had in my mind I was going to make enough money to buy something to eat. I did not know how much Mrs. Francis would pay me for cutting her grass, but if I could just make enough to buy a loaf of bread and some candy, I would be happy, I kept telling myself.

Mrs. Francis gave me a biscuit for lunch. I was glad to get that, because I had been working for hours and I was beginning to get hot from the sun and very hungry. I still had a lot of grass left to cut at lunchtime. It took me all day. I had to get use to using a sling blade, and I did the best I could. I was glad to finish, so I could see how much money she would pay me. When I told Mrs. Francis I was done, she told me to wait just a minute as she went into the house. I thought to myself, *she is going inside to get money to pay me.*

When she came back, she carried a large, brown paper bag full of her husband's neckties. He died a few years earlier. She hand me the bag and said, "These are for you."

I did not know what I was going to do with the neckties, so I told her that I thought I was going to get paid money. I had told my brothers and sister I would bring money home for them.

"Wait a minute," she said, went back into the house again. She came back and handed me a nickel. I really did not know what money was worth, but I knew I couldn't buy much with a nickel. I felt so hurt. I worked all day in the hot sun cutting her grass and cleaning her back yard. What was supposed to be a yard turn out to be a field, and all I got was a nickel and a bag full of neckties.

I cried, as I walked down the dirt road going home, carrying the bag of neckties. I did not want to take the neckties home, I had no one to give them to. I decided to get rid of the neckties before I got home, so, as I walked along the ditch of the dirt road, I began to string the neckties in the ditch, one at a time until all of them were gone. All the while, I cried. I felt hurt and confused. I worked for something I had no use for, a bag full of neckties. I took the nickel and bought peppermint candy for everybody at home.

The ride to New York gave me plenty of time to think. My mind raced with thoughts of the wood I had to cut for the fireplace during the cold winter months, all the washing by hand in a tub, drawing water every day from the well. No, there would be nothing to miss about Alabama, except Aunt Katherine. October would come quick and we would be coming home, but I wished we did not ever have to return to Alabama. I was tired of cutting wood and I was tired of washing, cooking and cleaning.

CHAPTER 4

UPSTATE NEW YORK AND THE MIGRANT LABOR CAMP

June 1959

IT SEEMED AS THOUGH we rode on the bus for many days, although it was only three days. I was anxious to get to New York. I heard some of the older peoples on the bus talking about New York, the tall buildings and sidewalks. I'd never seen a sidewalk. Some of the people on the bus had been to New York before. They came back year after year to pick beans. Everybody was just as happy as I was to get there. They had run out of food.

At last, we made it to Upstate New York late that Sunday evening, just before dark. Everybody was tired, but happy. It showed in their speech and laughter. I could not sit in my seat; I had to stand so I could get a better view of everything. It was just as I imagined. It was beautiful!

There were tall, metal poles with lights, all along the street. At last, the streetlights I dreamed about. My heart pounded fast, I escaped Alabama.

This must be heaven, I thought.

37

A tall, brick building stood at the corner of the street. A traffic light on the same corner control the traffic. I had never seen a building so tall; somebody had to explain what it was. I learned the tall building was an apartment building. After learning what apartment meant, all I knew was I wanted to live in a building like that.

Joe parked his car on the opposite side of the street from the tall, brick apartment building. The bus driver parked behind him. As I looked around from the bus window, I saw buildings all along the street on both sides, close to each other.

Joe stopped in the city because Cousin Betsy lived on the third floor – the top floor – of that apartment building. There was a club on the first floor; people stood on the sidewalk in front of the club. We could not get off the bus, because Joe said we would not be there very long, just enough time to drop off Cousin Betsy. Sidewalks, apartment building, all this was new to me. When I heard people on the bus talking about walking on the sidewalk, I finally understood. Since I sat by the window, I opened the window to stick my head out, but with all the excitement, half of my body hung out the window, while I looked as hard as I could at everything.

The smell of roasted peanuts filled the air; a man sat in front of the club selling roasted peanuts in small, brown paper bags. Joe stayed in town longer than he said. It started to get late, but no one cared. Everybody just sat, watching all the peoples on the street. The people were dressed up, better than I had seen people dress. Across the street from the apartment building I saw an area lined with nice cars parked in a big, open space. I heard somebody explain it was a parking lot. On the same side of the street where the bus parked, there was a place where many men sat and some hit balls with a stick. I learned it was a pool hall and they were shooting pool.

I had never seen so many people. I guessed all those cars belonged to the people in the club and Pool Hall. Only two people I knew in Alabama had cars. Whenever somebody needed a ride, we walked about two miles to ask for a ride. And it wasn't free. Many times, Mama had to pay to get a ride into town or to the doctor.

The music inside the club played loud and clear, loud enough for everybody on the bus to hear. I looked inside the large, glass window of the club. People danced, drank, laughed and seemed to have fun.

If only Mama could laugh and have fun, that would make me happy, I thought to myself.

Joe came out of the building at last, and the bus driver told us it was time to head to camp. He said it was another 20 miles away. I did know the camp, another new term, was the place we would live for the next four months. The bus driver followed behind Joe's car and we left the city. As we got farther and farther from town, it looked more like the country we left in Alabama. It was very dark. The only light came from the headlights of the car and bus.

Images of the city flashed in my mind as we got farther and farther away from town. I fell in love with the city, just that fast, with all those streetlights.

When the bus arrived at the camp, a scary feeling came over me. There were some people already in the camp. They arrived earlier on another bus. Joe was not the only migrant worker crew leader. Another crew leader brought buses with people from Florida and other parts of the South. I did not know who owned the camp. At first, I thought Joe owned it, but I later learned Joe was just a crew leader. The farmers who grew the crops owned the camp. They hired out for crew leaders who got the number of laborers needed for the seasonal work.

I could not see very much, but the area around the buildings was dimly lit. The bus stopped in the large, dirt yard in front of the buildings. As we unloaded the bus, Joe told everyone what to expect. Joe said they were there to work. Everybody on the bus had a room. If there was a single person, two people would share a room. There were rooms in the front and back of the building. Joe gave us a room on the end of the back building. The room on the end was supposed to be the biggest. Mama was the only person who had a big family, and all six of us stayed in one room.

There was one twin bed in the windowless room in the back of the building. Mama and my little sister slept in the bed, while I slept with my three brothers on the concrete floor. Joe gave us some blankets to spread on the floor. Joe said he would try to get us another twin bed, which he did after a few days. The beds were the only furniture in the room. I had always slept with my brothers, so nothing changed. I got a small corner of the bed on the end.

I awoke early to get outside of our room to explore what the camp looked like in daylight. I looked at the short, flat top building that had many doors. Behind each door was a room. I was not sure if I would like living at this place. It was not much different from what we left in Alabama. The other side included a yard with a big building. Inside the building was a big room with a Jukebox and a floor big enough for dancing. One side of the room was set with a few tables and chairs. There was a counter for food and drinks. I later learned the big room was the recreation room. It looked like they were adding onto the building. A place for cooking was next to that. There was another smaller building for washing clothes, and taking a wash up. It also contained the camp toilets.

After I finish looking around the camp, I was ready to go back to our room. As I walked back across the yard, I realized there were many small rocks in the yard. These rocks were not the same as the ones in Alabama. I later learned the rock was gravel. I had to get used to walking barefoot on gravel. When I returned to the room, I woke the rest of the family so they could see our new home.

The first day on the camp was a Monday, a rest day from the long ride. They would not start picking beans until Wednesday. Everybody got to know each other. Those who rode with us on the bus had gotten to know us, but the people who were already at the camp didn't know the new people yet.

The room next to ours housed two cousins, Fannie and Mae. It was their first time coming up North for seasonal work so Mama did not feel so alone having someone in the same shape. The only difference was they did not have children. They only had to take care of each other.

Mae was a short, fat, dark-skinned woman, who wore a headscarf on her head. She dipped snuff. She always spit in a can. Fannie was nice she was very quiet and wore a scarf like Mae. She acted just like a kid asking Mae for permission before she did anything. I felt good around Fannie because she acted more like me instead of a grown person. Mae and Fannie were probably older then Mama. My mama was the best-looking woman out of all the women on the camp. She was only twenty-seven years old.

Bob and Allen lived in the room next to Fannie and Mae's room. They met each other on the trip from Florida and got along good so they took a room together. These are the people we talked the most to our first few days on the camp, and they became like our family.

Joe provided a loan against wages to the workers who had no money. Joe gave Mama twenty dollars to buy food. She promises to pay him back when she started work. Joe did everything he promised Mama he would do before she left Alabama. He said he wanted us to be happy on the camp. I wondered where Joe would stay. He pointed his house out to Mama, across the field. It was a large, white house not far from the camp; Joe lived in it for the season.

The next day, Joe came back to the camp, after he had gotten some rest. Everybody needed some rest, after being on the road for three days. When he came back to the camp, he had a small woman and two teenagers with him. He introduced Mama to his family. Joe had a family! He had a wife, son and a daughter! I stared at him, trying to figure how he had a wife and Cousin Betsy was his girlfriend at the same time. I wondered if his wife knew he kept a girlfriend. Maybe she knew and did not care or maybe she knew and could not do anything about it. I was shocked and so was Mama to know Joe had a family.

Joe's wife was a small pretty woman but she looked sad in the face.

With the money Joe loaned Mama she sent me to the store down the road. I had to get something for us to eat. The store not far from camp did not have much food, but it was close. No one in the camp had a car. Mama gave me a list, things that would fill us up. There was no place to keep our food cold, so we had to eat a lot of bread and jelly, Vienna sausages and saltine crackers. In Alabama we ate a lot of biscuits and rice. We ate it for breakfast and supper. Sometimes we bought bologna when Mama got her welfare check. I never got tired of eating the same thing, I was just glad not to be hungry, but it would be nice to have some meat other than bologna. The days of making biscuits were over for me. We had to eat white bread. Mama made good biscuits, but sometimes I wanted white bread, or "light bread." Since she was working, I hoped we might eat white bread all the time. I was tired of making biscuits and I knew my brothers and sister would be glad they did not have to eat the dough biscuits I made.

After two days of rest, it was time for work. Everybody knew what Joe expected. "We're here to work," Joe said over and over to everyone.

The bus left for the field at six in the morning, so the workers woke up very early. I got up when Mama got out of bed, because I wanted to see her off to the fields. The bus driver parked the bus in the front of the camp and waited for the workers. There was a line at the bus when Mama got there. I promised Mama I would take care of the children, while she worked. I watched Mama as she stood in the back of the line, waiting to get on the bus, in a pair of old shoes someone gave her for work.

After the bus headed for the bean field, I realized nobody was on the camp, except me, my brothers and little sister. We were the only children on the camp. I began to get scared, since the rest of the kids were still asleep. Even though no one else was around, I felt like someone watched over us. I walked around the camp, as I had done the first morning we got there. I would rather be in town. I did not like the camp at all. There were so many woods close by, and the camp was set off the road. Mama did not tell me what to do if something happened with the kids. What if somebody who wasn't supposed to be there, came to the camp? What would I say or do? All I knew was I had to take care of my little sister and brothers. I figured it would be the same thing every day until October.

The first day alone in the camp was the longest day I could remember. The boys played all day. They played cowboys and Indians and threw rocks for fun. Tommy had a set of green plastic army men he played with, mostly by himself. I did not have to worry about him too much. He sat and played with his army men all day. I just made sure he was clean, because of his condition. I carried my little sister around on my hips most of the day. My little sister was tiny and I did not want her to get hurt.

The first workweek, Mama looked so tired and I was sad to see her so tired. I knew she was used to hard work; she picked cotton and worked in the fields all her life, even though Mama was sick a lot as a young child. My aunts told me Mama played sick when they were growing up, so she would not have to work in the fields as hard as the rest of them. It was up to Mama to take care of us. I hoped she did not get sick picking beans. Mama told me what to feed the kids during the day when they got hungry while she was at the bean field. I made them jelly sandwiches, when I could get them to stop playing long enough to eat. I do not remember eating. I was so busy making sure the boys did not get into trouble during the day. I wanted the day to end, so Mama could come see about us. Although I tried to act brave, it was scary being alone on the camp.

When the day ended and Mama came home from the bean fields, I felt a whole lot better. Mama waited to wash up because there were so many people using the sinks. Sometimes Mama waited for hours for her turn to wash up. It was the first time we saw a sink. In Alabama, we used a tin tub half-full of water to take a bath. During the winter we placed the tub behind the wooden stove to keep warm while taking a bath.

After about two weeks at the camp a dark blue car drove up in the yard. I was afraid but I tried not to show it. A man got out of the car. He must have known I was afraid; by the way I looked at him. I do not think he knew we were at the camp alone. He told me he was the inspector and had come to check the camp to make sure it was all right to house workers. I did not know what he was talking about; I just stared at him as he walked around checking everything in the camp. He walked around the whole camp as I had done when we first got there. He brought a pad and pen writing as he looked around. When he was finish he told me he would be coming back during the summer.

Every week, new workers came to the camp from the South to pick beans. One new worker, Jake, came after we were there for a few weeks. Jake took a liking to Mama right away. We liked him from the beginning, too. He seemed to be a kind man who treated us good. Jake was good at picking beans. Sometimes he picked thirty bushels in a day. On the weekends Jake gave us money to buy candy. It was good to have candy for a change.

I liked Jake, but I did not want Mama to have a boyfriend. I did not care about Papa any more. I did not like to call his name or think about him. I just wanted it to be Mama and my brothers and little sister; she did not need a boyfriend! I had not gotten over what happened with Silas, how he cut her arm. I never wanted her to have another boyfriend. I wanted Mama to be just ours – belong to just me, my brothers and sister.

It took a while, but I started to feel a little better about the camp. The children minded me during the day, or they knew they'd get a spanking. I started to feel special. I was in charge of the whole camp, while no one else was around. I cleaned our room, by sweeping the concrete floor and washed our few clothes. The days dragged on for me, but, as it got closer to the weekend, the time went a little faster. Even though the camp was dead during the day, at night, after everybody came home from the field, it was alive. People from town came to the camp at night. The jukebox would be playing and there was dancing, and card playing. I liked it when the people came from town; it made the camp more fun.

When the camp was full of people from the city, Jake came to our room a lot. He told us stories to make us laugh. We liked it, when he came to our room. Jake liked to play cards, so when there was no card game going on, he came to our room.

The men always found a way to get liquor on the weekend. The people from the city brought it to the camp, even though the camp was supposed to be dry. Jake drank he said, but he did not get drunk. There was one thing I did not like about Jake. He carried a knife, as most people did.

Silas got Mama's address and wrote her a letter. Aunt Katherine must have given him the address. The letter arrived while she was at work. I got so mad, as soon as I saw his name on the envelope. I opened the letter and read it. He told Mama how much he missed her, and how sorry he was for what he had done. He claimed he did not know what came over him. My anger grew as I read the letter. The vision of the night he cut Mama's arm came back to me. I tore the letter into little pieces and threw it away.

Mama never knew she got a letter from Silas. I never told her. I watched for more letters from him, thinking he would write her again, but he did not. Mama's sister Katherine did write Mama to tell her Silas had left Alabama and moved to Chicago. She knew Silas liked Mama, but she did not know he cut Mama's arm before we left Alabama. Mama never told any of her family what Silas did, and I did not tell.

Mama made a little money, not enough to buy us anything new yet, just enough for food, washing powder and her cigarettes. We used washing power not only to wash clothes, but also to wash our body. This way she didn't have to worry about buying soap.

As time went by, Jake became a bigger part of Mama's life; he helped her pick beans, so she made more money. The pay was fifty cents for a full bushel basket of picked beans. With Jake's help, Mama usually picked sixty bushels a week. After five days of work, that sixty bushel of beans added up to what seemed like a lot of money to me.

I was happy taking care of the children for Mama, until the day I let my little sister out of my sight and she climbed on an old tractor parked next to a building. She fell and cut her arm. I was washing a few clothes by hand and not paying attention to her, as she climbed on the tractor. She had a long cut on her arm that was wide open. The blood ran down her arm. She started to cry. I did not know what to do to stop the bleeding. I found a piece of cloth and put it on the cut. The bleeding did not stop right away, and I started to cry as my brothers stared at me.

After a while, the bleeding stopped. She should have gotten stitches, but there was no way to get her to a doctor. I did not know how I was going to tell Mama what happened to my sister. There was a phone in the recreation room, but I did not know who to call. Besides, I'd never used a phone.

I felt my sister's pain. I wished it were me who got hurt, instead of her. I could not stop her from crying. She was scared of blood. I held her in my lap and rocked her back and forth, until she cried herself to sleep. The boys did not want to play anymore. They just stood around us and watched my sister. I was mad with myself. I had been a good babysitter up until that moment. I just knew Mama was going to be furious.

It seems like that day would never end. I wanted somebody to come and help me. By the time Mama got home from the bean field, the cut on my sister's arm had closed up and it did not seem as serious as when she first cut it. Mama did not get mad at me. She told me I was still a good babysitter and she knew I would never let any of the children get hurt on purpose. Those words, coming from Mama, made me feel so good, but I knew my little sister would have a scar on her arm forever.

CHAPTER 5

MAMA GETS SICK

August 1959

IT STARTED TO RAIN a lot, toward the end of July. Nobody picked beans, because the fields were too wet. Everybody knew ahead of time, that some time it would rain, and the weather was not always good. The weather had a lot to do with how much money was made picking beans. My brothers and sister were glad to have Mama with us; they thought I was mean to them. Whenever they did something I believed was wrong, I spanked them. I had them under control until Mama was around. When she came back, they would not listen to me. Every evening she came from work, they talked all at the same time, telling her every time I had spanked them that day. She told them that I had better not do it again, just to make them feel better. She knew I did whatever I had to do, to get them to be good while she worked. It seemed Mama did not have the will to make them mind her. I was the one who made them behave. She let the boys get away with so much. I guess she felt sorry for them, because they did not have good clothes and shoes and no father in their lives. I didn't have those things either, but I was the oldest. I could take the hardship better.

On rainy days, many field hands hung out in the recreation room, where there were things to do, like listening to music, dancing and play cards. We sat in our room or went to the recreation room to watch the adults. They sold food and drinks in the recreation room. The word got around the camp, about my three-year-old sister dancing. She was a good dancer. Everyone wanted to see her dance. Usually, someone put her on the counter in the recreation room, so she could dance. The older folks liked to watch her. They gave her a nickel or dime to dance. My little sister had learned how to dance by herself. No one taught her. It was something that came naturally to her.

People from the city, especially the young girls, came to the camp on rainy days, looking for the men who lived on the camp. Some city people picked beans, too. A bus brought workers from the city in the morning to the bean field, and returned them to the city in the late evening. On rainy days, the workers from the city still found a way to come to the camp. They had made friends with many people on the camp. So, they stayed in the camp all day, dancing and having fun. More and more people from the city came to the camp. They liked it better than the workers who lived there.

With nobody making money, the workers in the camp got uneasy and angry at each other. Everybody was getting along, until they had too much time on their hands. The camp people argued a lot and wanted to fight each other, but they did not because Joe warned them against fighting.

As the weather improved and people went back to work in August, everyone living in the camp became happy again. Mama grew sick while picking beans that month. She took sick right after all the rain stopped. Mama did not know why she started to get very bad headaches and feel sick all the time. She told me when she felt sick, but claimed all she needed was some rest. Mama needed to see a doctor, but there was no money for medicine or a doctor. It got harder and harder for Mama to pick beans. She missed a day and tried to work a day. It was too much for her, so she could not pick beans anymore. However, we needed to stay in the camp until the bus left for the South in October. We had nowhere else to go and no money.

Mae came up with the ideal that Mama could cook for her and Fannie, while they worked in the field, and they gave her a few dollars to help her along the way. They felt sorry for us. Jake gave her money to cook for him, too. Mama was a good cook. She was happy to get whatever money she could. I knew I had to help get some money for us.

Even after October, there was nowhere for us to go. I was sure someone else lived in the old house we left behind. Mama never told Mr. Robert we were leaving, and she did not paid the rent before we left. She left before she received her welfare check.

Now that Mama was not able to work in the field, I wanted to go for her. I was used to work, because I helped my Aunt Katherine pick cotton. She took me to the cotton field and let me pick cotton alongside her. I carried my cotton sack over my shoulder to put the cotton in, and would pick until I had a half sack full of cotton. Then, Aunt Katherine added what I had collected to hers. I liked to go pick cotton with Aunt Katherine, because the driver of the cotton truck stopped by the store, so the cotton pickers could grab lunch before going into the cotton field. Aunt Katherine always bought me a honey bun and a can of Vienna sausage. I had to help Mama; it was just her and I to take care of the other children, with no family in New York except Cousin Betsy. We only had each other. Mama did not want to let Cousin Betsy know she was not working.

I had an idea, so I ask Mama to buy me a pair of tennis shoes. I knew she did not have money for shoes, but a pair of tennis shoes cost only a few dollars. If I got a pair of tennis shoes, then I would be able to pick beans in her place.

I ask Joe if I could go to the field, since Mama could not work. Joe did not want me to pick beans. He said I was not old enough and he would get in trouble, if I was caught working in the field. "They don't know how old I am," I told Joe.

Joe said I was supposed to be older before I could work in the field, but he never said how old. Only a few peoples knew I was only eleven years old. At last, Joe agreed that I could pick beans, but I had to be careful not to get hurt. Even though I was only eleven years old, I was big for my age. I could easily pass for fifteen or sixteen. Joe always treated us a little better than the rest of the workers. I think it was because of Cousin Betsy. Also, he knew we did not have anything, and any help was good.

Mama gave me three dollars. I went into the city with Fannie and Mae. They had a ride with a friend from the city they met while picking beans. Tennis shoes were the cheapest shoes I could get. Since I didn't have any shoes with me, I went into the city barefooted. There was a shoe store on the corner across the street from Cousin Betsy's apartment. I walked into the store to see how much a pair of tennis shoes cost. I wanted a black pair to work in the field. A white pair would get too dirty from the bean field, but I really liked the white pair. As it turned out there was no black pair in my size, so I had to get a white pair. Two pairs of tennis shoes cost five dollars and a single pair cost three dollars. I had just enough money for one pair.

It was my first trip into the city since we arrived in Upstate New York. Everything was prettier than I remember. I was glad to be in the city. The streets looked different to me. Where Cousin Betsy lived was a busy part of town, in the heart of downtown. There were more buildings then I remembered. There were a furniture store, a small grocery store and a liquor store right down the street from her apartment. All of the stores had apartments on the second floor above them. There were many other streets with houses, churches and stores. Men sat on the sidewalk near the liquor store, with their wine bottles. I counted three clubs on Cousin Betsy's street. I saw men and women drinking moonshine when I lived in the South, but this was the first time I'd seen men drunk sitting on a sidewalk. Of course, it was the first time I'd seen a sidewalk, too.

While in the city, we stopped by Cousin Betsy's apartment, which was on the third floor. I had never been in a building three stories high: Climbing the stairs to her apartment, I felt a little nervous; I had never seen so many stairs. There were nine apartments in that building, three on each floor. In Alabama, all the houses that I saw were wood, so brick buildings were new to me. Cousin Betsy's apartment was nicer than any place I'd ever seen. I wanted to stay with her forever. I wanted to move in with Cousin Betsy, with Mama, my brothers and sister, too.

I knew it was too much to hope for being that it was so many of us, but I hoped in my heart. Cousin Betsy had everything she wanted and needed because Joe supported her. Cousin Betsy did not come to the camp too often. Joe spent a lot of his time in town at her apartment, when he was not working.

The building Cousin Betsy lived in had something black on the outside I had never seen before, a fire escape. She said it was used to escape the building in case of a fire. Each floor of the apartment building had access to a fire escape. Cousin Betsy tried to get me to stand on the fire escape, so I could see everything going on down the street. I did not want to be that high up from the ground, so I decided to stand on the steps of the building to watch people.

The club on the ground floor of the apartment building was the same club I saw peoples dancing and having fun the first evening we got into New York. The Jukebox blasted songs I have never heard before. The song in the North was different from what I heard in Alabama. I was used to listening to songs like "Jailhouse Rock" and "Sweet Home Chicago." As I stood in the doorway of the apartment building, I spoke to everybody who passed. In the South, people spoke to each other, so I did the same thing in New York. I did not know the people up North only spoke to people they knew. As I spoke to each person, he or she looked down at my feet. I did not know why, until a woman came up to me and said, "little girl, we don't go barefooted here."

That was the first time I found out people in the North did not go barefooted, as they did in Alabama. I believed people went without shoes everywhere, if they wanted to, not that I wanted to, I just didn't have any shoes yet. In the South, even the adults walked around in their bare feet. I only owned the pair of tennis shoes I just bought to work in. I did not see anything wrong with going barefooted. After the woman finished talking to me about going barefooted, I went back upstairs to Cousin Betsy's apartment and put on my new tennis shoes. My eyes began to fill with tears. I did not want to cry, but the tears would not stop coming. It was so easy for me to cry. I was always crying about something. I felt something was not right. New York was supposed to be a better place than the South, but the people acted mean. I began to feel sorry for myself, thinking the hardship we had in the South followed us up north.

I was still happy not to be in Alabama. I wanted Cousin Betsy to say Mama could come and move in with her, it seemed like too much, but I continue to hope.

I was up early Monday morning and got ready for the bus to go to the bean field. The bus left you if you were not out there on time, and I did not want the bus to leave me on my first day. I was so happy about going to the bean field. I had heard how much fun it was, and, at last, I was going to make some money for Mama. I did not know how to pick beans, but I was ready to learn. *I bet it's like picking cotton*, I kept telling myself.

The workers got the rows of beans they wanted to start picking. Everybody got two rows of beans. Mae got two rows of beans for herself and got the row next to her for me, so she could show me how to pick. She told me that I should start with a single row.

I wanted two rows like the others. I did not know if I could pick two rows at a time, but I wanted to try. Fannie got the rows on the other side of me. She showed me how to get on my knees between the two rows and pick from one row, then pick from the other row until all the beans were picked. I started moving up the row on my knees, picking from side to side. I could see some workers had kneepads and I soon found out why. I thought my knees were coming apart, but I did not let anybody know. I just had to get used to working on my knees.

I talked to Fannie on one side of me, and Mae on the other side. There was a girl name Ellen who picked beans before and was two rolls over from me. This was her second year coming from Florida. She was much older than I was, but she was closer to my age than anyone else working. She helped me fill a basket. Fannie and Mae threw some beans in my basket.

There were workers from another migrant camp picking beans in a field close to where we were picking. I heard them singing as they picked beans. I loved to sing. I started singing when I was very young. I sang to myself as I worked. The time went by fast. I had to pick beans very fast if I wanted to make some money. The workers from Florida were good at picking beans. They had done it for years and could finish two rows before I knew it. I was only halfway down my rows, when everybody else started new rows of beans. I hoped to pick a lot, but I soon learned it took a lot to fill a bushel basket.

The morning was not so bad, but around noon, I had parched lips, throat as dry as a desert and knees indented from the rocks. With the sun beaming down, sweat flowed down my face into my eyes and blocked my vision, until I wiped the sweat away with the sleeve of my shirt. No matter how hot it was, everyone wore a long sleeve shirt, for protection from the sun and bugs. I kept working, no matter how hot it got. Nobody else seemed to notice the heat, so I was not about to complain. Every evening, after getting off work, I scrubbed my knees, but I soon learned the marks on my knees were there to stay. Mama made me a pair of kneepads, but I could not keep them on my knees. I worked better without them, so I gave up on kneepads.

All the full bushel baskets of beans were between the rows for weighing. Each full bushel basket of beans had to have the exact amount of weight before we got a ticket worth fifty cents. Once we reached the end of the rows, we counted the bushel and called the weight person over to weigh our beans. I learned fast that I had to watch the full bushel basket of beans I picked, because somebody would sometime steal your full bushel in your row, if you were not paying attention, and put them in their row. It was hard to work and I kept looking back to see if somebody stole my beans. Getting a ticket from the weigh person was such a good feeling! I felt like I had done something good. After each ticket, the feeling became stronger.

There was a truck parked away from the field where they sold food. The food truck included a stove. Almost everybody used his or her first two tickets for a sandwich and soda. Smoke Sausage on two slices of bread, with mustard and ketchup was everybody's favorite. I looked forward to getting a sausage sandwich. I worked better after I ate something.

I did not have any breakfast. There was no food for breakfast. Mama did not have enough food for breakfast, only enough for supper. My brothers and sister ate white bread and jelly during the day.

The first few weeks, I picked about four bushels a day. I kept telling myself I would do better the next week. We worked until almost sundown and then got on the bus to head back to the camp. I made up my mind that picking beans became easier with each passing day. I didn't have any other choice. The workers sang and talked. They filled the fields with laughter. I could not wait to get to the field each day, even though it was hard work. I was glad when the week was over, so I could turn in my tickets for cash. Sometime I lost a ticket before because it was time to collect the cash. That was such a horrible feeling. All tickets were cashed in on Fridays at fifty cents a ticket. It was the happiest day of the week. Everybody had some money, after such a hard week of working.

Even though the season was more than half over, we had new workers arriving at the camp. I do not know how they got there, because there was no new bus coming from the South. All the men came from different parts of the South. Mama kept cooking for more and more people. The men arrived without wives to cook, so they were glad to hire Mama. The little money I made, I gave it to Mama.

Most of the young men were of very dark complexion, with gold on a front tooth. To me, they were very cute. The girls in the city came to the camp at night, even after picking beans all day, just to see the young men. None of them were serious. It was just a fun thing. They knew at the end of October they would go back to their families. Many of the young men were married with a wife and kids back home.

Joe tried to control the workers he brought from the South. He hired workers to help him with the running of the camp. He came down from his house all the time during the night on the weekend, to talk to the state troopers, who were called when there were fights. Joe was the only one the officers talked to before they arrested somebody, since he was the overseer of the camp. Joe warned everybody on the camp, many times, there would be no fighting. He threatened that anybody fighting would be forced to leave. The people from our camp did not start fights much. City folks started the fights. The city people felt they could come to the camp and take over. I thought it was why they liked to come to the camp. I don't know if they felt they were better than us, but it seemed that way.

There was gambling all the time, especially during the weekend when they stayed up all night. I heard music playing while I was in bed. I started to dislike all the drinking on the weekend. There was supposed to be no drinking, but the people from the city continued to bring the liquor, even though they were warned. Somebody from the city always ended up getting kick off the camp after fights. It seemed to me everybody carried a knife. Somebody was always getting threatened with a knife and my nerves were very bad, because of Mama getting cut in Alabama. Troublemakers could not come back to the camp. If they returned, Joe called the officers. Joe's job was not easy, even though he made lots of money. It was hard to control the camp. The more workers kicked off the camp, the more new people arrived from the city with liquor.

Jake was left handed and word travelled around the camp that he would cut people. He was quick as lightning with his left hand. He drew his switchblade knife before you could blink. One weekend, a man tried to talk to Mama and Jake got in an argument with him. Jake cut the man and end up in jail. He did not stay long, because it was self-defense. Joe got Jake out of jail and allowed him to stay on the camp. He had promised anyone in trouble would have to leave the camp, but Jake was one of the best bean pickers in the camp.

During the summer, Bob and Allen became the best of friends. Bob was a tall, young man who was kind and would help any of us. He took up time with my little brothers, taking them for walks and playing ball with them. Bob became Mae's boyfriend; they spent a lot of time together. Fannie found a boyfriend at the camp, too.

Allen was just like a kid. He played around a lot with everybody, never making any money picking beans. Allen had not grown up yet. He had a nice brown complexion and a big smile, but he was always bothering people. Allen did not have family with him, so whoever had food fed him. He liked it when Mama cooked and shared. We started to get better food to eat. Allen played jokes on people and got the biggest kick out of it. As soon as he got back to the camp from the bean field, he started playing. Everyone had a lot of patience with Allen, even though no one wanted to be bothered with him. Allen was more than eighteen years old. Others on the camp talked about Allen throwing rocks while people worked. Joe warned him if he got into any more trouble, he'd be sent back to Florida. I liked Allen a lot. He made my brothers and me laugh. Allen came home from the bean field and started to play around with Bob. Bob chased him into the woods behind the camp. One day, Allen kept playing with Bob and Bob chase Allen into the woods. While Allen was in the woods, he found a rusty, old knife. He started playing with Bob with it. Bob warned him to not play with the knife. Allen made a mistake and sliced Bob's shoulder. Someone rushed to get Joe to take Bob to the hospital for stitches. Bob ended up with thirty stitches. The police came and took Allen to jail. Bob did not press charges, so Allen left jail the next day. Everybody knew it was an accident, but Joe was tired of Allen and kicked him out. Allen gathered his belongings and Joe took him to the Greyhound bus station. He bought Allen a ticket and put him on the bus back to Florida. We were very sad to see him go. He cried, because he did not want to go back home. Bob did not have any hard feeling toward Allen for what he had done.

A lot happened in the camp. The summer flew by and everybody worked very hard. I grew used to the camp. I was used to picking beans. We would head back to Alabama soon. I started to feel sad, because I did not want to return. There wasn't time to think about Aunt Katherine or the rest of the family in Alabama. We were busy trying to survive. They did not need to know the hardship we experienced. I knew we could not stay at the camp any longer than October, but I kept hoping there was a way for us to stay. Without heat in the rooms, by October the weather would be cold and staying would be impossible.

Cousin Betsy and Joe began to not get along. He became very jealous. After all, she was very pretty, and he did not want her to go anywhere. Joe spent more time with his wife and children. Joe's wife picked beans with the rest of us. She looked sad all the time. I thought Joe was mean to her. She must have known Joe had a girlfriend. Joe's wife left and went back to their hometown, about forty miles away, before the season ended. His two teen children stayed with him.

There were still quite a few beans to be picked, even though the season was nearly over. The rush to finish began. I heard the men brag about how many bushels they picked each day. It was like a game to see who picked the most. Jake was always one of the men who picked the most. I picked five bushels a day. Jake and Mama grew very close. He treated us like his family. During the week, he worked very hard. On the weekend, he liked to play cards. Jake was a good person, but if he got angry, I knew he might cut somebody with his knife.

October raced toward us. There were only four weeks left for picking beans. Joe said anyone who wanted to stay longer could remain and pick white potatoes, but they would have to move into the city. Some of the workers started to look forward to going back home, but not us. I still hoped we would not return to Alabama, but I knew we did not have anybody to stay with, once the camp closed. Mama began to worry. She knew we could not live in our old house again.

Joe spent more time away from Cousin Betsy. He went home to his wife on the weekends. His son and daughter knew about Cousin Betsy. They seemed to love her. She cooked for Joe's children, as if she was their stepmother. I do not know if they got along with their mother, but it did not seem fair to their mother that they would spend time with Cousin Betsy.

October arrived; everything wound down. All the beans were picked and everybody started thinking about going South, wondering what was next. The bus would leave the first Sunday in October. We had arrived on the camp on a Sunday in June and were set to leave on a Sunday. Mama got our few things together for the trip back home to Alabama. We only had the few clothes we came with in June, nothing new, except my tennis shoes.

Suddenly, my brother Tommy became very sick. It started the Friday before we were to leave. Mama took him into the hospital emergency room in the city. Joe gave her a ride. Tommy had been lucky so far. He had not been sick since we came to New York, but now he was very ill. Mama didn't have money or insurance but the hospital did not turn away Tommy. The doctors said he had to stay in the hospital. Tommy had a fever of one-hundred-and-three, and he felt a lot of pain. His large intestine swelled because of an infection and he needed an operation. The small intestine never gave him any problem. It was always the large intestine when we were in Alabama. The doctors in the emergency room called in a specialist from another city to perform the operation. They had never seen a condition like his before. Tommy underwent his operation the Saturday before the camp closed. Joe finally said he would take all of us to Cousin Betsy's house. Mama stayed at the hospital with Tommy, so I got my brothers and little sister together, so Joe could take us to Cousin Betsy's apartment.

The bus was scheduled to leave Sunday; the bus could not wait for us. We could not leave until Tommy got better, and nobody knew how long he would be in the hospital.

CHAPTER 6

LEFT BEHIND

**Upstate New York
October 1959**

THE BUS LEFT EARLY Sunday morning without us. As much as I thought I wanted to stay in New York, I did not want it to be this way. I felt scared, like we were stuck up North, without our family. I wanted to go home. I began to cry for Aunt Katherine. I thought about all my cousins and Grandma Lillie. For the first time since June, I missed home. It confused me when I wondered how we were going to survive. I had to be even stronger for Mama, my brothers and sister. I became the backbone of the family.

A few workers stayed to pick potatoes. These men found girlfriends in town they lived with in the fall. Jake moved in with Cousin Betsy, along with us. He did not want to leave Mama, knowing Tommy was sick. I do not think Jake had anything to go back to in Mississippi. Jake said he would pick white potatoes as long as he could. Tommy's illness scared me. He had been sick many times in Alabama, but this time was different. We'd always been surrounded by family when Tommy became sick, but this time it was just Cousin Betsy. Tommy's operation went well. The doctors who operated moved his intestines from the center of his stomach to a spot closer to his right side. His intestines were not as swollen right before his surgery, and even smaller after the operation. The doctors told Mama that Tommy would need many more

59

operations, with the plan was to move his intestines a little closer to his side until it was in a better position for him. After Tommy's operation, he wore a plastic bag over his intestines to hold his body waste. This turned out to be much better for him, and easier on me.

Before the plastic bag method, I changed his diapers. Even though he was growing up, he wasn't able to pin the diaper. The only problem now was getting the plastic bags. It was the first time I had heard a word for Tommy's surgery – colostomy. What we had gotten use to calling "The Thing" had a name. Colostomy, a word I never forgot, explained a condition that overtook his life because of his birth defect, something he lived with forever.

I had always taken care of Tommy, and only wanted the best for him. He was treated in the children's ward of the hospital, where the nurses fell in love with him. He was such a cute little boy with big curls in his brown hair, the nurses gave him many gifts and toys, even the visitors who came to visit other patients fell in love with Tommy. They brought him toys. Before long, Tommy had more toys than he could play with. The doctors told Mama he would not be able to travel for a long time; he was so weak from his operation. The doctors wanted him near the hospital, so they could check on his condition. The doctors had done an operation on Tommy that had not been done on anyone else in the area. With the many operations that followed, they wanted him to remain in New York.

With Tommy in the hospital and no money for us to live on, Cousin Betsy suggested Mama go to the welfare office. Mama went to the welfare office for help. She was turned down right away. The caseworker at the welfare office said she was sad for us, but the only help they would give was medical care for Tommy while he was in the hospital and once he was well enough to travel, they would give Greyhound tickets for all of us to get back to Alabama. Mama explained to Tommy's doctor what the caseworker said. The doctors were not happy at all, so the doctors gave Mama a letter to take to the welfare office, stating Tommy needed special medical care and could not ride a bus back south. Mama took the letter to the caseworker, and they said her case would be reviewed again. They said she would have to wait for the review and did not know how long it would take. Tommy stayed in the hospital for three weeks.

Joe took the workers back South. He planned to take it easy during the winter months. His children left for home, to join their mother, when he took the workers back to Florida. We settled into Cousin Betsy's apartment, but it was very crowded. She really did not want all of us in her home. She was not happy with so many people. At first, she tried to be kind, but then things were not good at all. Every day she changed toward us. I imagine she realized Mama had no one else for help. Cousin Betsy said we brought down her standard of living. She lived well, with Joe's help, but he stopped giving her as much money. I do not know if he quit giving to her because we lived with her or because the season ended. He visited her on the weekends, but they were not getting along. Not long after Joe came back from Florida, he and Cousin Betsy broke up for good. He returned to his hometown, wife and children.

I silently promised we would pay Cousin Betsy back for everything she provided us. She became so nasty with Mama, I just wanted to leave. She fed us, gave us a place to sleep, and we were thankful.

The weather turned cold. My brothers, sister and I needed warmer clothes. School started in September in New York. Tommy and I were old enough to attend. I could not go to school, because Mama did not have money to buy clothes and shoes. Besides, she did not know how long we would be in New York. Tommy had never attended school, even thought he was seven years old, because of his health issues. I never started school the beginning of the school year in Alabama. For some reason, Mama sent me after Christmas. I wanted to go to school. Mama never had to force me go to school in Alabama. As soon as I received shoes for Christmas, I was ready.

It seemed we were not going back to Alabama for a while, so I started fifth grade, with the help of Cousin Betsy. She bought my first real pair of shoes – a pair of pink, patent leather shoes. I felt in love with those shoes at first sight. Cousin Betsy let me choose the shoes I wanted. It was my first experience with a pair of pink shoes.

The school was a large, white concrete building, with shiny, wood floors. The school contained classes for first through sixth grades. All of the teachers were white. In Alabama, the kids were black and the teachers were black. I had never been around white kids or a white teacher before.

My earlier school years were in an old, one-room school house. The teacher was an old black lady who fell asleep during class. She was my mother's teacher when she was in school. I started taking the school bus in the fifth grade. The school was eight miles away. It was the only school for black children. The most I remember about the school was lunch.

The change was not easy for me, because of my southern accent. All the black kids made fun of me because of the way I talked. I did not talk the way they did. They claimed I talked funny. I wanted to be friends with my classmates, but they only made me cry. Because I was used to black kids, I wanted them to be my friends. I wanted someone to play with, but they had too much fun making jokes about me. Whenever I had money to buy candy, I shared with some of the girls in my class, especially the ones who made fun of me. They took my candy and still made fun of me. My mind closed. I could not learn. The North was so much different from the South. I did not have to go without breakfast anymore during school, as I did before. I received free breakfast at school, which was oatmeal and milk. The fifth and sixth grades I had free breakfast. I had to walk to Cousin Betsy's house for lunch. She gave me a sandwich, and then I walked back to school. Lunches were served in the school cafeteria for those who had money. Once in a while, I got to eat lunch at school. The lunch food in Alabama was different from New York. I was first introduced to tomato pie and pizza in New York. It was something I never heard of, but grew to like. I hated going back to school after lunch, because of the other kids in school. Once I was in class, it was not so bad; it was just during recess time I felt all alone. The changes from the South to the North so far, had not been good.

The lesson I learned at the young age of eleven was that "Somewhere Else" would not make our lives better. It was up to me, and all I wanted was a chance and a little luck. No matter where we lived, I would make it. I would help Mama make it with the rest of the children and I knew I had to finish high school, no matter the odds. I had no clothes or shoes, but if I went to school, one day I would buy clothes and shoes for my family. I promised myself that I would get a job as soon as I was old enough. I needed lunch money and food for my family. We were on welfare in Alabama, and finally on welfare in New York. I did not want to receive welfare all the time. I did not care when I picked beans. I hoped to set an example for my brothers and sister. The hardship I endured made me a strong person.

We suffered, but now I suffered with a goal, to make a difference.

Jake picked potatoes for a little while, and then he looked for a job. It did not take long for him to find a real job; he was promised a job at the slaughterhouse, killing cows. Before Jake could start, he needed a pair of rubber boots and union dues. It cost twenty dollars for boots and twelve dollars to join the local meat cutters union. Jake lacks the thirty-two dollar to get what he needed to work. I wanted so much for Jake to get the money, because I knew this was our chance to move out of Cousin Betsy's apartment. No one had money, except Cousin Betsy, so he borrowed it from her. He liked his job a lot. Jake promised Mama he would find a place for us to stay as soon as he could. Even though Jake found a job, I still hoped Mama would get welfare assistance, because it would be too hard for Jake to take care of all of us. I was also scared Jake might leave us, just like Papa. Welfare would mean more safety. However, I promised myself that, as a grownup, I would not accept welfare.

After a lot of paperwork and appointments, we were back in the welfare system. A check came in the mail a month before Mama knew what it was. She put her mail away, not realizing she had a check. We had been suffering and had money, and did not know it! The check Mama received was the most money she ever had. It seem like it was so much money, at that time. Mama started to get welfare checks, and she and Jake began looking for a place for us to live. It was difficult to find a place big enough for five children. Jake promised me he would buy me some new clothes, once he was on the job for a while, but not until we got settled into our own apartment.

Jake found a place for us. It was in a rooming house, two buildings down from Cousin Betsy. The red brick building had an upstairs and downstairs. I did not want to live in that building, because I heard people talk about it, calling it the "The Bum Building." It was where all the bums and wine heads lived. Mama and Jake knew the rooming house was where wine heads lived, but it was the only place they could find for us, so we had no choice.

Once we moved, we met an older couple living in the rooming house, Mr. and Mrs. White. They were delighted to have children in the building and were quite kind. Mrs. White took a liking to Tommy. She gave all of us food and goodies, but Tommy got a little more than the rest of us.

My brothers and little sister was too young to know we lived with bums. They were happy to be free to play and have fun. At Cousin Betsy's place, they got into trouble.

The men in the rooming house drank a lot of wine that only cost fifty cents. When they became drunk, they slept on the steps, in the hallway, wherever they could find a place, but they never bothered us.

We had two rooms – one room was big enough for a bed and dresser, the other room was only big enough for a bed. Jake, Mama and my baby sister slept in one room, my brothers and I slept in the other. We shared a kitchen and bathroom with the other tenants. We were the only children in the building, until another family moved in with two little girls. Everyone in the building got used to us. They began to love Mama's kids. We became friends with all of them, and they were like family to us. The so-called bums looked out for our safety. They would do anything to help us and were our friends. Living in that building was the first time Jake and Mama had an argument, and he drew his knife on her. I pled with him to put the knife away, and he did. It would become a habit, him pulling his knife on Mama.

School ended in June; it had been a year since we arrived in New York. I looked forward to the sixth grade. I could not wait to get my report card. When my report card was given to me, I had failed the fifth grade and would repeat it. I was so mad that last day of school. I was scared to go home and tell Mama I failed. After all the trouble I had getting used to a new school and having kids make fun of me, I ended up failing. Nonetheless, I knew I had to finish high school.

Tommy continued getting sick every few months, his intestines swelled and he went back into the hospital again, and again. The only thing that helped him was to be in the hospital. He had surgery again after a year; his colostomy was moved again, closer to his side. The hospital and the doctors got to know him very well. I walked to the hospital to see him after school every day. Mama did not like to go visit him that much, so it was up to me. Each time he went to the hospital, he came home with many toys. I did not have to take care of him as much as when he was younger. He learned to take care of himself.

After living in the rooming house for a year, Mama managed to get a larger apartment in Cousin Betsy's building. We moved across the hall from Cousin Betsy. That apartment building was in the heart of town, everything happened within those two blocks. It was a four-room apartment, which was nicer than living in the bum building. Jake continued to live with us; he made good money at the slaughterhouse. He helped the family a lot. I got new clothing for school. It seemed things had improved for us. Everyone had a good time in the city. I forgot we were poor. Plenty of money was going around, people were happy, and Mama was happy, too. Cousin Betsy moved to an apartment down the street. We moved into her old apartment, which was larger than the one we were renting.

The State of New York said that Tommy had to be in school. He did not fit in very well with the other children, and they laughed at him because he wet his pants and had no control of his bowel. It became so bad that Mama kept him home. The state approved for him to have a tutor come to the apartment. Miss Wesby was a short woman who walked with a limp. She was born with a disability of her own. She and Tommy got along well. She taught him to read and write.

After living up North for two years, someone gave Mama a copy of a newspaper called *"The Pittsburgh Courier"*, in the paper was her name. Papa had put an ad in the newspaper "Looking for my wife and four children." His name was listed, along with his telephone number. I counted to myself, there were five children. Papa did not include me, and I felt hurt. Even though I was four years old when he and Mama married, he was the only father I knew. I thought he cared about me. He treated me like the rest of the kids, until he tried to mess with me. That is the day Papa died in my mind and heart.

It was just as well Papa did not include me, he was not a good father anyway, but he was the only father I knew. I still wanted a father. Mama did get in touch with Papa after reading the newspaper ad, to let him know where we were. Papa explained to her why he put the ad in the paper. He wanted her to sign divorce papers. He found another woman and wanted to get married again. He sent the papers to Mama. She signed the papers and sent them back to him. She did not have any regrets about the divorce.

The city was booming, and there seemed to be a prosperous time. Crime was everywhere; there was much sin in the city. Migrant workers continued to come from the South to pick beans, but we never saw Joe. There were several migrant labor camps in the area. During the bean picking season, the workers from the migrant camp came to town on the weekend. Someone was always being shot or cut. The word around town was that people from Florida did not play. If you fought with them, someone got hurt. It was nothing to look out of the window from our third floor apartment and see two men dancing around in a circle with knives cutting at each other. My fear grew stronger with each passing day, especially on the weekend. I could not stand to hear anyone arguing or talking loud. The cuss words that came out of the mouth of the people made me very nervous.

Jake started to go out more and more. He began to come home late at night drunk. He always wanted to argue and fight with Mama. She argued back. I asked her to be quiet, but she refused, ignoring me. There were even times he took out his knife at her, and I would jump in the middle of them, pleading with him not to hurt her, my heart racing and knees buckling. Jake lowered his knife. He started to listen to me, but Mama continued to run her mouth, angering Jake even more. Once again, I had to be afraid for my mama. I do not know why he started a fight with her. She never went anywhere, always home with her children. It seemed as though Jakes punished Mama for the wrongs he committed. Eventually, Jake moved out and went to live with his girlfriend, who he had all along.

Mama found out she was going to have a baby. When Mama told me, I told her I was moving out of the house, because I was not going to help her with more babies. She told me to move if I wanted to, but she said it with sadness. I was thirteen years old and tired of taking care of children. I had nowhere to move to except, in a cubby hole off the hallway of our apartment. It was only a threat I made to Mama because I was hurt about her having another baby. I wanted to make her feel bad. It was five of us already, and it was hard on me, being the oldest, because I felt responsible for the younger children. We barely had enough food, not to mention clothes for my brothers and sister.

Jake moved back with us after being gone for a short time, it seemed to me he was going to change, but it never happened. Mama gave birth to a baby girl, Sarah, who I loved a lot. I did everything I could to help Mama with her, as I continued to help with the other children. Jake was back to his old ways. He continued to threaten Mama on the weekends, when he drank. I never knew if he was serious, but I never gave him a chance. I was always between them. I never got much sleep on the weekend, because I knew Jake wanted to fight with Mama. Even though our apartment was on the third floor, I heard Jake as soon as he started climbing the stairs on the first floor. I got out of the bed and waited for him to wake Mama and start arguing. I hated weekends because I hated the feeling of fear, and not getting any sleep.

A few years later, Mama had another baby girl, Jean, who I loved as much as the others. Now, Mama had seven children from the ages of fourteen to a newborn. I stopped complaining about children, because I could not do anything about it. There were seven of us. Jake left us again, he moved in with a new girlfriend, Beverly. Jake still bought things for us sometimes; he visited during the week, he gave Mama money if she asked for it. All of us loved Jake a lot, but I was afraid he would hurt Mama someday when I was not around. I was glad Jake had a new girlfriend, because it meant I could get some sleep on the weekend.

Jake's new girlfriend had friends in our building. She came to visit them and managed to always be loud when she entered the building, so Mama knew she was around. She knew Jake had lived with us, so whenever she saw Mama, she taunted her about Jake. Mama never said anything, but I knew she was hurt. Beverly was different from Mama. She drank liquor and cursed a lot. She was like Jake. She carried a knife, like Jake. One day, Beverly stepped on Mama's foot as she passed. Mama went into our apartment and got a knife after Jake's girlfriend. She swung the knife at her, but missed. I pleaded with Mama to put the knife away. "This woman is not worth going to jail," I reminded Mama. Jake's girlfriend never said anything else to Mama after that incident. Jake stopped coming around as much as he did before and we seldom saw him anymore. He left some clothes at our house, and Mama threw them out the window. When Jake saw his clothes on the sidewalk, he ran up the stairs to the third floor. I waited, because I knew he had his knife out for Mama. I begged him, holding his hand that held the knife. "Please, don't cut Mama," I said.

I knew it would not be the last time Jake pulled his knife out, because whenever he did come around, he and Mama argued. Once again, he pulled his knife out at her. I was so tired of jumping between the knife and Mama. I argued with Jake whenever he and Mama got into it.

"I do not play with children," he always said, but my plea was always heard by him, not to hurt my mama.

Mama did not get her copy of her Divorce Decree until four years after she signed the papers. Even though Papa had left the family in Alabama and gone to Pittsburg, the divorce papers stated that Mama had committed "willful and malicious desertion and absence from the habitation of the injured and innocent spouse, without a reasonable cause" therefore his divorce was granted.

One Sunday morning, the news went around town that a man was killed at a bar the night before. The bar was down the street from our apartment. The man who got killed we knew from walking down the street every day. We did not know who killed the man until later in the day, when somebody told Mama that Jake killed a man. It shocked all of us to discover Jake killed a man. I knew, one day, he would hurt somebody.

Jake had a reputation with his knife, because he always drew his knife on someone. Jake was fast with his switchblade. We learned Jake got into a fight with another man and accidentally killed an innocent bystander with a knife. The innocent bystander Jake killed tried to get out of the way, several men held Jake's arms to keep him from fighting. He had his knife in his left hand. As the innocent bystander attempted to pass to get out of the Jake's way, Jake snatched his left arm from the grip of the men who held his arms and the innocent man was stabbed in the jugular, as he passed Jake. He died instantly.

Even though it was an accident, Jake was going to jail. Jake ran and left town. He disappeared into thin air. There was an all-points bulletin for his arrest. The cops in the city had no idea where Jake went. Word began to spread that Jake had left town and was staying in another city. Mama discovered where he was hiding, when one of his friends gave her a message on a note. "Please come to help me" it read, with the address of his hiding location. With no transportation, she had to find someone she could trust to take her to Jake. She decided to talk to a minister, the Reverend Smith, who she and Jake knew. The minister said he would drive her.

Jake was hiding in the basement of a family he knew ninety miles away. Mama and the Reverend Smith persuaded Jake to turn himself in to the law. It was not easy to convince him, but he finally decided it was the right thing to do. Mama and the minister took him to the police station. There was no way Jake would return to his hometown in Mississippi. I felt sad for him, but I was also very glad I would not have to worry about him pulling his knife again. I could get on with being a fifteen-year-old teenager.

Jake waited in jail for a long time before his trial. His trial lasted for weeks. We would not have any help from him while he served time in prison. It would be a long time before we saw him again. The judge sentenced Jake to seven years. Even though it was an accident, he still got prison time. There was sadness about Mama, after Jake went to prison. With seven children to take care of, it became harder for Mama to feed us. She worked house cleaning jobs when she could and picked strawberries several times. I knew I would have to find a way to earn money for my family, especially during the winter months. I knew I could pick strawberries in the spring. During the summer, I picked snap beans.

Strawberry season started before school was out. I went to the strawberry field on the weekends. I was good at picking strawberries. I usually picked forty of the quart baskets a day. Picking strawberries was not so different from picking beans; all of it was hard on the knees.

I loved going to the bean field. Many young people caught the bean bus when it came into the city to pick up workers. No one cared how old we were. I got used to picking beans from my days on the migrant labor camp. None of the young people knew that I once lived in the camp. I put my days living in the migrant labor camp in the back of my mind.

I needed to make some money during the winter months, so I asked people if they needed their houses cleaned on Saturdays. I did ironing for two families to get money. All the money I earned went to Mama for the household, except a dollar or two, which I kept to buy myself something. I loved to buy magazines. I bought magazines about singers and movie stars. It was my dream to become a singer one day. "Just maybe I could become a movie star, too", I told myself.

CHAPTER 7

MAMA'S DEPRESSION

Upstate New York
1963

MAMA COLLAPSED INTO A state of depression when Jake went to prison. She was not the same person. She was sad all the time. She quit cooking for us and never left the house.

There was a storefront church three buildings down the street. At 15 years old, I went to church. Mama did not tell me to go to church. I felt the need to be a part of a church because it was something in my heart I wanted to do. I began singing in the choir, which made me feel special. I was good at singing. I became a choir leader, because of my voice. I dreamed of becoming a singer when I finished high school. I decided I would go to Motown and become a famous singer. Singing was my way of forgetting about the daily trials in my life. Even though I struggled through poverty, my focus was on the future. Whenever I thought of my family's living condition, a little bit of joy entered my heart, as I thought of becoming a singer and changing our living condition.

I spent a lot of my spare time in church. Even though we'd lived in New York for quite a few years, I had not made many friends. Church was my only joy; Sunday's was a long day in church. It seemed like Reverend Smith would never finish preaching. He was a large man, with a voice that echoed throughout the church walls. I always wondered

71

why it took him so long to preach. Was it because he thought God did not hear him at first?

I finally got Mama to go to church with me. She was just becoming active in the church, before Jake went to prison. She loved working in the church. After Jake went to prison, she stopped going to church. I wanted my mama back. Even though I was the backbone of the family, I still respected my mama and I did not know what was going on in her mind, why she was so lifeless, but I was going to be there for her no matter what. I could not understand what happened to her. She started to let my three brothers have their ways; she did not spank them anymore. They did mischievous things.

My brother Tyrone got so out of hand; he stole bicycles from other kids all the time. I knew I had to do something about his stealing, so I threatened to take him to the police station if he kept stealing. The threats did not stop him, so one day I grabbed his hand and pulled him to the police station. The police station was a few blocks up the street from our apartment. He cried and pulled away from me, but I was stronger than he was and he was going to the police station, even if I had to drag him. When I entered the police station, I explained to the police officer why I was there. I told him Tyrone had been stealing bikes. The police office told me he would take care of everything. He took my brother and showed him what a jail cell looked like, and talked to him about theft. He put so much fear into my brother, until I felt a little sorry for bringing him. Tyrone was seven years old when I took him to the police station. The fear the officer put in my brother was enough to keep him from stealing bicycles for a little while.

I was the one who gave my three brothers spankings in the past. Even though Tommy was ill most of the time, he still got spankings from me. My middle brother Thomas did not get many spanking from me. He was more concern about eating. So long as he had something to eat, he did not get into trouble. Mama left it up to me to take charge of my brothers. She continued to have a weakness when it came time to disciplining her boys. With her depression, she just did not care what they did. Therefore, I had to do what I believed was the right thing to raise them to be good children.

When I came home from school, Mama was sitting, staring out the window. She had not started supper for us. It was as if she did not care anymore. I cooked supper for my brothers and sisters. Usually, I had to find something to cook. We always ran out of food before the month ended. Even though we did get government surplus food each month, it did not last the entire month. So, each month, I missed school to stand in line to get surplus food, which was cheese, power milk, rice and canned meat, The canned meat was either spam or canned beef. The only thing we liked was the cheese and rice, but we ate everything.

We did have a charge account at a small grocery store down the street from our apartment. There was a certain amount the owner, Mr. Kelly, allowed us to charge each month. Once we reached that amount, he would not let Mama charge anymore. We were completely out of food by the second half of the month, the grocery bill reached more than a hundred dollars a month quickly; after all, it was seven of us, including Mama. Once we went past a hundred dollars, Mr. Kelly would not let us charge anymore. He was afraid he would not get all his money on the first of the month, when the welfare check arrived. Mama asked Mr. Kelly if she could charge a little more for the month and he always said no, once he told her no, it meant I would have to go and plead with him to let us charge more food. Mr. Kelly did not give in to easily, but he eventually said okay. He made me promise that once I reached a certain age, I would be with him. I was fifteen years old. He liked me a lot, but I was too young for him. "Girl I can't wait until you get older," he said, with that devilish look in his eyes. I did not care what he said. I just wanted groceries.

The seventh and eighth grades had been the hardest for me. I did not always have lunch money, nor did I have any breakfast to eat before going to school. The hardest thing was to have to stop by the bakery every morning for my teacher to get a fruit bar. My seventh grade teacher, Mrs. Johnson, knew I had to pass a bakery to get to school. She loved fruit bars and asked me if I would stop by the bakery on my way to school, to get her a fruit bar. She gave me twenty cents to get her fruit bar. A hungry, little girl in a bakery in the morning with the smell of fresh baked pastries and bread was more than I could take. I came out of the bakery hungrier than when I entered. My teacher offered me a piece of her fruit bar, but I never accepted. A fruit bar was not very large. The first two weeks of the month, I made a sandwich for my lunch, but after those weeks were over I was back to being hungry again. It was hard to learn on a hungry stomach.

In the seventh grade, there was a book, *Little Britches*, we read every morning in reading class. It was a story about a farm boy who worked very hard on the farm and before and after work, his mother made great meals. Just by reading, the description of the homemade biscuits and pies his mother made for him was satisfying for me to read. I could not wait to begin reading the book each morning. I got lost in that book. I could taste the food, and it was as if I was eating with them.

I applied for a summer job when I was fifteen years old. I lied about my age and claimed I was sixteen. I stopped going to the bean field. The migrant workers still came from Florida to pick beans, as they had in the past. I wanted a real job. My first job was at a motel, cleaning rooms doing the summer months. They said I could work on the weekends during the school year. It was going to be good to have money and be able to buy for the rest of the family. My first paycheck was forty-two dollars. I added up my hours all week and kept coming up with forty-two dollars. I was sure it was a mistake. To think I was going to make forty-two dollars was more than I could believe. When I finally got my paycheck, I was thrilled. It was forty-two dollars. The first thing I did every week was buy groceries for the house. I saved the rest for school clothes. By summer's end, I had saved enough money to buy some school clothes. I was in high school and wanted to dress better, and eat lunch each day.

Having a job was the best thing I could have done for my family and me. It seemed my life was nothing but work, but that was good for me. I learned the importance of working for a living. We still were not getting enough money on welfare for the things I needed. There was never any money left from our welfare check to buy me any school clothes. Occasionally, I got something new on the first of the month. If anyone got something new to wear, it would be me, because I was the oldest.

Mama began not to worry so much. She got used to the fact Jake would not be around for a long time. She saw I was able to help her more, now that I worked a real job. As long as she had her Pall Mall cigarettes, she was somewhat happy. I made sure she had her cigarettes. When she did not have any cigarettes, she became very angry with all of her children.

Even though she was somewhat happy she still refused to leave the house. My family needed to get another place to live. I was ashamed of our apartment. I never let any of my friends come to my house. We did not have good furniture. All of our furniture was quite worn. Mama found our furniture at the Salvation Army. The building that was so beautiful when we first arrived in Upstate New York turned out to be mice infested. All nine apartments needed work done. As the time went by the building changed, the property owner would not make repairs.

After starting high school, I made friends, because of my witty attitude, and I loved to make people laugh. I sang for them. I began to have fun. I had some decent clothes to wear and I was passing in school. I was too young to go into the clubs, but my friends and I hung out on the corner of the street, and watched people as they went into the club on the first floor of our apartment building. We walked up and down the street peeking into the windows of the three clubs on the street. Not everything seemed so bad in my life. My friends asked me to join a sorority. I was president for one term. Even though there was a period in my life when I had fun, I learned as a teenager that" somewhere else" would not make our life better. It was up to me to make the difference.

I did not know our apartment was so bad, until I visited my friends' houses and saw how they lived. All of them had nice apartment, and they lived in the housing project. My friends' homes were warm and comfortable. That let me know we needed to do better for ourselves. I had nothing to compare our living condition to before, because anything was better than what we had in Alabama. I believed it would help Mama with her depression to have a new place to live, but she was so unwilling to leave the apartment. So, once again, it was up to me. I persuaded Mama to apply for an apartment in the housing project. We were promise an apartment when one became available, and put on the waiting list. When an apartment became available, Mama did not fill out the required paperwork to get the apartment, therefore, we lost that apartment. I cried when we lost the apartment, so I visited the housing commissioner and asked if he would give us another chance at an apartment. He put us on the waiting list, again. After a few months, another chance came for us to move into the housing project. The housing project I preferred was close to where we lived, and was where all my friends lived, but it did not have any vacant apartments. The only apartment available was on the other side of town. There was no way we were going to lose that apartment, even if it was on the other side of town.

I lived a long way from my friends. I even had to change schools. The only transportation was by city bus and the buses stopped running after dark. I missed my friends a lot, a place in the housing project was worth it. We did not have to worry about heat in the winter, which was the most important thing. A new stove and refrigerator came with the apartment, and that was something we never had before. To move into the project made me happy. The apartment was a lot nicer than where we lived before. "Maybe we can get new furniture," I told Mama.

I was seventeen years old when we moved into the project. Living there equaled living in a mansion for me. I got a bedroom to myself for the first time in my life. For once, I felt secure.

No one told me how important an education was. Finishing high school was my goal, but I never considered college. I knew I would not be able to go to college. A high school diploma was as good as going to college to me.

At the beginning of my final year of high school, I got a job at a laundry. I went straight to work after school and worked eight hours. I kept this up for six months, but it was too much for me to attend school and work full time. Finally, I decided I could not let anything get in the way of me graduating. I suffered too many years to fail. The last year of school went fast. I had no plans for my life, but I knew I wanted to leave home. I did not want to be with my family anymore. Although I loved my mama, brothers and sisters, I wanted my own life.

I waited so long for graduation day. I felt I accomplished one of my goals in life. I endured the sadness, pain and suffering, with a diploma as my reward. With my diploma, I was determining not to depend on the welfare system. I could do better for myself, but Mama was stuck. She tried to work, but she couldn't always find a ride, or she got sick. Even if she did work, it would have been harder on me, because I watched the other kids. I planned to continue helping my family. Even when I did not live home anymore, Mama would be a priority.

Graduation day turned out to be very sad. Mama and I walked together to my high school for the ceremony. It wasn't far from the housing project. I was glad Mama attended my graduation. I went to my sixth and eighth grades graduations alone. The sadness overcame me when I realized I had no other family members around, except my brothers and sisters. They were too young to appreciate my achievement. No one cheered for me when I walked across the stage to get my diploma. I realized how much I missed my family in Alabama. Yes, I had my diploma, but suddenly I felt scare and alone. How I wished I had a celebration like the other students who graduated.

After the ceremony, Mama and I walked home. I did not get a congratulations or hug from her, but I hoped she was proud of me. She would not have cared if I dropped out of school. There was never any encouragement from her. She did not realize the importance of finishing high school. Even without the encouragement I needed, I knew dropping out was never an option. I was the oldest child in the family and the first to graduate from high school, including the family left behind in Alabama. I was proud of myself. I'd already worked most of my life. Now, I hoped to get a better job. I took up office practice and typing in school. The greatest thing I did was learning to type. I became quite good. Typing was an asset in the clerical field.

My dream to become a singer never became a reality. I never created a plan to make my dream a reality. When I realized I was not going be a singer, I began to hyperventilate and cry. My dream of becoming a singer had all but vanished. I had no time to think about a real plan, I was too busy trying to help my family survive. I evaluated my life and asked myself, *where do I go from here?*

The only reality within my reach was for me to finish high school and always have a job. Without a plan, my dreams remained just that, dreams. At least the dreaming inspired me during my teen years; I needed those dreams to ease the everyday pain of my life. I became restless at home; I married soon after high school, and left Mama with six children.

I was not happy in my marriage. I regretted leaving my family. I was the one who took care of them for so many years. Yes, I needed a life of my own, but my life remained secondary. I should have stayed home a little longer to finish raising my brothers and sisters. Once I married, my heart ached because I could not see them every day, I wondered if they had food. I found it hard to sleep. My mind flashed back to the Saturday of my wedding, the sad looks on my family faces as I left home. I could not help them as much as I had in the past. Being married changed things. I had no money to give Mama.

Jake was released from prison a year early, because of good behavior. By the time Jake came home I had graduated from high school, was out of the house and married with a child of my own. He moved in with Mama and the children. They were glad to have him back. I felt good Jake moved home with Mama and the children. I felt he would help her. The two children Mama and Jake had together were small when he went to prison. They did not know him very well, but it did not take long for them to love him. He got his old job back at the slaughterhouse and he and Mama were happy together. He bought things for the children and made sure Mama had what she needed to run a household.

About a year after Jake left prison, Mama became pregnant, so she and Jake got married. They named their baby boy Rod. It was strange having a baby brother younger than my own baby. Jake and Mama's marriage lasted a few years. Even though they live together off and on for years, they never had a stable relationship. The happiness disappeared, and Jake cheated on Mama, as he did before he went to prison. He started going out a lot on the weekends, but he did not want to fight like he used to before he killed a man. I think it was because he was on probation and did not want to return to prison. Gradually, it got so bad between them, that he moved in with another woman and her children. After Jake left, he quit helping the family. I imagine he took good care of his new girlfriend and her family. He never stopped by to see his children, though he passed by the apartment all the time.

My baby brother, Rod, never got a chance to know his father. Everyone was so sad when Jake left the family. I felt sorry for Rod. He really needed a father. My other three brothers were used to not having a father around, and my sisters were more attached to Mama.

Jake lived with his new girlfriend until he got off probation. Then he decided to go back to Mississippi. I loved Jake as a father and I appreciated the help he gave us when we first met him, but he played a major role in my life because of the fears he caused – my fear of knives, and the fear of loud cussing and arguing. Jake lived with his mother in Mississippi. He never wrote Mama, but his mother stayed in contact. She wrote and told Mama the things Jake did in Mississippi. Jake lived a reckless life, without care in the world. Mama never got over losing Jake. Whenever we talked about him, the sadness showed on her face, Jake never returned to New York State.

I wanted more for my brothers and sisters, but only a few of them finished high school. They did not have the ambition I had to finish school. The struggle continued for most of them, as they became adults. Four of my siblings married and had children. They moved away to other States. I struggled. I made some wrong choices in my early adult life. I was married at nineteen and at twenty-one, I had three children. I got divorced after seven years of marriage. With the divorce came freedom to once again help my mother financially as I had before I got married. I was always blessed with a job. If I knew how to change fate, I could eliminate a lot of the pain in my life, but not knowing how to do that I have to make the best of life even when the pain remains.

WHEN THE PAIN REMAINS, PART II

Upstate New York
October 1993

AFTER MAMA'S CANCER WAS diagnosed and her surgery performed, the doctors kept her in the hospital for more than a month. It seemed they were not in a hurry to release her from the hospital. Student doctors began visiting along with the cancer specialist; I think they used her as a learning tool for the interns. I visited her daily and applied lotion to her feet for her, trying not to show my sadness. I could tell she enjoyed it so much when I put lotion on her feet. As long as I could remember her feet had never felt soft, but now that she was sick they were as soft as a baby's bottom. I talked to her about happy things to make her feel better. We prayed together. I told her how much her neighbors missed her.

I kept asking Mama if there was something she wanted to tell me. I wanted her to give me instructions as to what she wanted me to do during her last six months. I wanted her to feel comfortable confiding in me while we were alone in her hospital room. I wanted her to talk to me about what she had gone through as a teenager; I needed to know her feelings, what she had felt during her teen years but she said there was nothing she wanted to talk about to me.

I tried many times before to get her to talk to me about her life as a teenager, giving birth to me when she was sixteen years old, without anyone's knowledge. I could not imagine the fear and pain she went through to give birth to me. I loved her for it, especially after I got over my teen years and knew the truth about my birth.

I pitied her and wanted to know her feelings. She must have been so afraid of her mother, to keep such a secret. I felt very sorry for any meanness I showed during my own teen years. I loved her for what she went through by giving me life. I wanted to hear it from her; I wanted to hear her side of the story. Even though her sister had told me, I would never hear it from her. I asked her again, if there was anything she wanted to tell me. She repeated herself again. "No," she said.

———————

When I was old enough to know I had a scar on my back, I asked Mama what happened to me. She said I got the scar as a baby. She claimed her baby sister made a mistake and scalded me with hot water. I believed the story until I became a teenager, and was very concerned about the scar on my back.

Aunt Gloria was always my source for family history. I visited her in Massachusetts during the summer, when I was a teenager. One summer day, I asked my Aunt Gloria what really happened to me and how I got the scar on my back. She told me everything, but I always wanted to hear it from Mama; I wanted to hear her words.

One day, as a teenager, I became so angry with Mama, because I could not wear halter tops in the summer. I was too ashamed of the scar. All young girls wore halter tops in the summertime. I wanted Mama to hurt as I was hurting that particular day, so I told her my aunt had told me about the scar. There was a sadness that came over her. "Did she tell you about Charlie?" Mama asked.

Charlie was Mama's youngest brother. The two oldest brothers joined the military before I was born and I did not get to know them well. Aunt Gloria had told me the whole story about Charlie and the scar on my back. I wanted Mama to tell me about Charlie. I wanted to hear the story from her.

Aunt Gloria said Charlie was mischievous as a young man and always in trouble. He was only a few years younger than Mama. The story Aunt Gloria told me was that Charlie and his best friend, Harry, who had a crush on Mama, were playing around one night. Charlie allowed Harry to rape Mama. She didn't tell the rest of the family at that time. The rape had been a secret only Charlie knew about. She became pregnant and kept it a secret. Neither her parents nor her sisters knew about her condition, until the day after she gave birth alone.

One night, she hid underneath the family home and gave birth. There was a lot of space underneath houses in the South. Houses sat on tall pedestals of stone. She gave birth without anyone's knowledge or help. When the morning arrived, she hid me in the woods and went to work cleaning house for a lady. During the day, her two younger sisters walked in the woods and heard a baby crying. As they followed the crying, they came upon a baby. My aunts picked me up – I was lying on some tree branches, wrap in old clothing. They brought me to their mother; I was covered with ants and a mark from the indentation of the tree branches on my back. When their mother saw me, she knew right away whose baby it was.

When Mama came from work, Aunt Gloria said she told them everything that happened to her from the beginning. She swore she was coming back to get me.

As I grew, the scar on my back grew. That is why my Grandma loved me so much and I loved her, she had nursed me back to life as an infant. Everyone in the country knew about the baby born underneath the house and hid in the woods. Aunt Gloria said my real father did not want anything to do with me. She said his mother made him go into the Army after I was born. I understood why Harry's mother sent him to the army; I never got to know him before he died.

There was a time, as a child, when I wanted a present father, but, as I grew older, I realized I already had a father, in God.

I wanted to know what was going on in her mind, what was Mama's plan for me? Was she coming back to get me, like her sister said, or was she just leaving me in the woods to die?

I just wanted to hear the story from her mouth. The foolishness about the clothes I could not wear because of the scar on my back passed in my life. It did not matter anymore. The scar only reminded me how blessed I was to be alive after being in the woods. Only heaven knew for how long. I shudder to think of what might have happened to me as a newborn infant – the snakes, the animals that could have ended it all for me. The hands of God saved me. Just thinking about that let me know that I am a miracle. No one realized that but me, and every day I am reminded by the scar that I carry. That is why I strongly believe in miracles.

If I had a dollar for the many times people have asked me, "How did you get the scar on your back?" I would be rich. As a child and as an adult, the question came up often. During the many years of going to doctors, they asked me, too. It was always hard to tell the truth when someone asked, because they would not believe me anyway, if I told them the truth. I always make up a story. Sometimes, I said I had surgery, or I was burned as a small child. Several times, when asked by a doctor what happened to my back, I told the truth and was looked at as if I was mentally ill. It hurt so much growing up with the scar, but now I can look back and be thankful I made it to where I am today.

Mama told me she needed boots to wear home from the hospital, because it had gotten very cold. I knew she would never get to wear them, with the swelling in her feet after surgery, but it's what she wanted, so I went to the mall and got her a nice pair of boots. She could not wear the boots, she did not have the strength to lift her feet to put the shoes on, and therefore she gave them to me. She mentioned she wanted to get some skirts and blouses, too. I told her that I would get them for her as soon as she was better and out of the hospital.

Thanksgiving passed and Christmas was approaching. Since, Dr. Martin was her main doctor, I pleaded with him to release her. I wanted to get her settled before Christmas. I wanted her last few days on earth to be pleasant. I wanted her to be with family during the Christmas season. How I wish I had told Dr. Martin not to perform surgery on her, she was never the same after surgery. She could barely walk or stand. After pleading with Dr. Martin to let Mama go home, he understood the situation, and said he would release her the next day, providing they could draw blood. I returned to the hospital early the next day to get Mama ready to go home. As it turned out, getting blood from her was hard for the nurses. They could not find a vein. The nurses did not give up trying to find a vein. I began to pray in silence, because I knew she would not be released if they did not draw blood.

After waiting and praying for what seemed to be hours, blood was finally drawn; she came home December 6. Mama was very weak and was unable to move around without assistance. She had loss all of her strength and would never walk alone again. The nurses put her into my car, but I had to get a neighbor to help me get her out of the car into her apartment.

Mama was delighted to be home again, even though it would only be for a short time. I took her to Massachusetts immediately. There was no one to take care of her. Sarah could take responsibility of caring for her. She was a trained nurse's assistance. She was not working at the time. I would have taken care of Mama, as I always had, if I did not work. The rest of my brothers and sisters were living in other cities, except Tommy and he could not care for her. Tommy lived with Mama. He was not well himself. She always felt sorry for Tommy, because of his condition. It seems to me she believed she was responsible for Tommy's condition.

I made a reservation for a U-Haul to move Mama's belongings to Massachusetts. Packing her belonging was one of the hardest things to do. Mama cried as she watched her things packed away into boxes. She wanted to take some of her furniture and the mementos she gathered during the years. I could not understand why she was so concerned about her things at the time, but I was glad she took the things that were dear to her. Moving some of her belonging to Massachusetts with her made leaving her apartment a little easier. She asked me what I wanted out of her belongings. The only thing I took was a painting of a windmill. She truly loved the painting, and I knew it would always be safe with me.

She lived in the same apartment for thirty years. She had not accumulated a lot. What little she did have, she was fond of it. The things she was attached to the most were the things I moved with her. Through the years, my sisters and I brought her household items that she was not able to buy for herself. She always cherished everything we gave her. I loved to buy for her. I knew what she liked, because of all my years shopping for her. She was not a hard person to please, anything and everything pleased her. It was sure to bring a smile to her face, whenever I gave her gifts.

Mama left some of her thing in the apartment for Tommy. He continued to live in the apartment they shared, until he could find somewhere else. He would have to move into a smaller apartment eventually, but he wanted to be independent, so this wasn't a problem for him. We moved into that apartment when I was in the tenth grade. All of Mama's children grew up in that apartment, which had four bedrooms. Everyone had left home, except Tommy. The apartment was too large for two people. Mama should not have been allowed to live in such a large apartment, but because she had lived there so long, the housing official let her and Tommy stay. After Mama left, Tommy would not live there for long. Tommy would be lost without Mama. Even though he loved her, there were times he argued with her and said things to make her feel bad. It appeared he blamed her for his condition. I know that, through the years, it had to affect her to see him so sickly and in the hospital most of his life.

There were times Tommy and I did not get along well as teenagers. He had a bad temper all of his life and I think that came from him being sickly. I knew he never forgot I was the one who took care of him as a child even though I was a child myself. Tommy thanked me many times for that care. I often wondered what he would have done if I had not been around to take care of him.

Many neighbors came to say their goodbyes to Mama, tears in many of their eyes. Word spread fast that she had cancer. I was surprised at the number of people who said to her, "Mrs. Louise, I heard you have cancer." I wanted to get angry with these people for saying that to her, but then I realized their lack of understanding about her illness. Everyone was shock about her illness. Mama's doors were always open to all the young people in the neighborhood. There was a basketball court across the street, in front of her apartment building. When young guys wanted a cold drink of water after playing basketball, they came to her house. They felt welcome and comfortable, knowing she did not mind. It was hard for everyone to imagine her not being in that apartment.

I took the day off from work to drive Mama to Massachusetts in my car; I followed the U-Haul truck toward Massachusetts. Someone close to the family drove the U-Haul. Mama had tears in her eyes, as we left the city she came to thirty-five years earlier to pick snap beans. We only intended to stay from June to October. We grew to love Upstate New York. We tried to escape the memory of the Old South. Things were hard in New York, but we never thought about moving back to Alabama. Her sisters would write and ask her to please come home.

Mama always said she never wanted to go back to the South to live. I told her the south was not the same as when we left it. Things had gotten much better; peoples had new homes, cars, and good jobs. I went back to the South several times and could see the changes. Even though there were many changes in the South, I never wanted to go back to Alabama, too many bad memories. Most of our family down there had died, except two of Mama's sisters. seven siblings died at young ages. My beloved Aunt Katherine died before I could see her again, when she was forty-two years old.

It was a bright, cold day when I drove Mama to Massachusetts. I tried to make conversation with her, but she just stared ahead, not saying much at all. I never let her know that I knew she had only six months, at the most, to live. She never said the word cancer. Perhaps she tried to protect my feelings. The doctor told me he had told Mama she only had six months, at the most, to live, but she never once said anything about what he said to her. To be in denial about one's illness is a tragedy in itself, and that was what happened with Mama. The word cancer seemed so final to me, I cannot imagine how it must have felt to her. Instead of saying the word cancer, she told me the doctors said she had "that thing." Even though she was leaving behind a life she once knew, to her cancer was not the reason. I continued to talk to her. "Once you are better you can get another apartment," I promised. I told her these things to get her spirit up, but I knew I was deceiving her. I knew no other way to cheer her up. I wanted to give her hope, and she needed a positive attitude to cope with the difficult days ahead of her, with that type of cancer.

She began to respond a little to my words, after telling her the things she could do with her life once she got better. She mentioned to me again, as she did when she was in the hospital, that she wanted to get new clothes, especially skirts and blouses. I promised I would get those things for her once she got better. It sadden me to know she would never get to wear the clothes she so desired. She never had many clothes. I bought her a new dress for special occasions. Once my sisters became of age, they bought her clothing. She had a love for shoes, but she never had many. Whenever we bought her new shoes, she gave them away if someone asked for the new pair. Cousin Betsy asked for her shoes and Mama gave them to her. Mama loved Cousin Betsy, even though I do not think Cousin Betsy loved her back. I always felt we were indebted to Cousin Betsy for helping us leave Alabama.

Arriving in Massachusetts, it looked like a snowstorm had just left the area. Large snow banks were everywhere. The snowplows had plowed the streets and left piles of snow along the side of the streets. The difference in the weather from Upstate New York to Massachusetts was a swift change. I noticed Mama had begun to cry again. As I approached Sarah's house, she sobbed louder and murmured at the same time. "I want to go back home! "I could not keep back the tears myself, because I knew I was bringing her to Massachusetts to die.

Convincing Mama the move to Massachusetts was for the best, I told her I would come to visit her often and would call every few days. Once she got inside Sarah's house, she stopped crying. She did not want her grandchildren to see her cry. The grandchildren knew Grandma was ill, but none of them knew what was wrong.

She was special to all of her grandchildren. When my children were growing up, they always wanted to stay with grandma. I had to force them to come home with me; I never wanted to put my children off on her. She never said no to them, when they wanted to spend the night with her. Mama had been by babysitter for my children until they started school, so I could work. I depended on her to babysit for me, but I never wanted her to do anything free for me. I paid her. I realized I was in a better position to earn money.

The money I paid her was the only money she could earn. She wanted to be able to work so badly. However, she couldn't hold down a job. Arthritis, along with diabetes, had gotten so bad, that there were times she could not walk. She sat in a chair by the window to watch her grandchildren play outside.

She received Social Security Supplement to take care of herself. To have the things she wanted in life, Mama knew she needed a job. We received welfare for many years; therefore, she was glad to get Social Security, because it was a little more money than what she received from welfare. She only received four hundred and thirty two dollars a month. Out of that, she had to pay rent, buy food and pay utility bills. After she paid everything, and everybody she owed money, she was broke within a week, and she would have to wait until the first of the month again.

By Christmas, Mama was settled into her new surroundings. Sarah did everything she could do to make her happy, but happiness would never be for her. The holidays made her miss home even more. Christmas had always been a special time for Mama. She could not give all of her children presents at Christmas time, but she made the best Christmas dinner for the family. Mama never had money for Christmas dinner, but somehow, someway, at the last minute, she received a blessing with what she needed to prepare dinner. This would be a Christmas she did not have to worry about finding money to prepare Christmas dinner.

To me, no one could cook as well as Mama. She made cornbread dressing and candied yams that melted in your mouth. She made the best sweet potato pies in the world. Everyone in the neighborhood knew when she made sweet potato pies. Someone unexpected would always stop by at dinnertime and Mama would feed him or her, even if there were only enough food for her. She was always the last to eat, even after cooking for hours. She did not mind if she did not get anything to eat, as long as she fed someone who was hungry. She was just that kind of person.

Decorating for Christmas was one of the other things Mama loved. She decorated her front windows so beautifully, with what little decoration she had. She never had money for a Christmas tree. I do not know if she prayed for a Christmas tree or not, but someone always gave her a tree a few days before Christmas. For Christmas as children, we were at the mercy of whoever wanted to give us something. The best Christmas we ever had as children was the time a family adopted us. They bought clothes for all of us, and toys for the younger children, and they gave Mama Christmas dinner for the family.

The family was determined Mama's last Christmas would be her best. We aimed to make it a special one that would be remembered for the rest of our lives. This was the last year Mama would be with us. Mama was not able to stand and help Sarah with the preparation of dinner, but she made sure everything was prepared the way she would have prepared dinner. There was laughter and singing of Christmas carols. The family forgot, for a moment, Mama was terminally ill. She told me she wanted a wrist watch for Christmas, which I got for her. She was so proud of that watch. Her eyes had gotten so bad she could not see the hands, but she wore it every day.

Mama knew everything I bought for her was from the heart. I wanted so much to make up for the hand life so wrongfully dealt her. I felt good when I did something good for my mama.

One of the best Christmas presents I gave her was when I bought her a new living room set. The furniture store delivered it to her apartment without her knowledge it was coming. That was one of the happiest times I ever saw her. My happiness was equal to hers.

January turned out to be a very cold month; the snow seemed like it would never stop, especially on the weekends. Sleet and freezing rain made it impossible to go to Massachusetts to visit Mama as much as I wanted. The entire month of January passed before I knew it. Mama did not want me to drive when the weather was bad, even though she wanted me to visit. Every time I talked to her on the phone, which was often, I could tell by her voice she was getting weaker. By the first weekend in February, the weather was still snowy, but I had to see Mama, so I took a chance and drove to Massachusetts.

Hospice was called to come help Sarah with her. The last week in February, Judy, a retired nurse, was assigned to help with Mama. She was a special woman who enjoyed helping others. She picked up Mama's medicine from the pharmacy; bathed her and helped her dress. Mama became so weak she gave up on doing things for herself. Even in her physical weakness, her will power was very strong. She continued to talk about the skirts and blouses she wanted.

A female minister who worked with hospice visited her once a week. She asked Mama how she felt about death. She said comforting things to her. She wanted her to understand what she was going through and to let her know God loved her. The people from hospice became very special to her within a short time. It was the first time I really acknowledged the volunteers of hospice as being the greatest peoples on earth. I knew it took special peoples to volunteer for hospice, but I really did not know how caring they were.

Mama's will power to live kept her going as long as she did. She was in so much discomfort. The morphine had to be increased to alleviate the pains she experienced. She wanted to be there for the birth of her first great-grandchild who was due the first week of March. Mama had so many small grandchildren and she would not be around to watch them grow into adults. The fact she was having a great-grandchild was the ultimate joy, at this time in her life. The baby girl middle name was Louise, after Mama. She was able to see the great-granddaughter born the first week in March. Mama was so proud of the baby, but she could not hold her. It seemed she waited patiently for that child to be born, before she went home to be with the Lord.

The times I talked to her on the phone, I realized I'd never heard anyone with the determination to live she had. She continued to talk about plans for the future. She talked about things she had never mention before, things she wanted to do with the family. If only we could get back all the years that have gone. I wondered if we could have made better choices, with so little resources.

As the time went by, whenever I heard her voice, it sounded lighter and lighter. She was very sick, but she still would not utter the words cancer or death. The third weekend in March while visiting Mama I noticed she vomited a lot. She acted as if her vomiting was normal. I suggested she go into the hospital for a few days. Mama said she wanted to get some things in order before she left for the hospital. I said she might not have to stay long and she could get things in order when she felt better even thought I knew she would never feel better. The pain she experienced had become more frequent. Many times she told Sarah she didn't need anything for pain, but Sarah gave her medicine anyway because she knew Mama was suffering. Mama did not want us to know how much pain she felt. The doctor said that the main thing to do for her at that stage was to make her as comfortable as possible.

After spending the third weekend of March with her, I returned home to Upstate New York. I asked Sarah if she would take Mama to the hospital early the next day. Monday morning, Sarah took Mama to the hospital. Sarah noticed how weak she had gotten. The doctor admitted her immediately. Sarah called to let me know Mama was in the hospital. I called her hospital room and talked to Mama briefly on the phone the day she was admitted, telling her I would be back to see her on the following weekend. She sounded weak over the phone. I had no idea it would be her last week. I called and talked to her Tuesday, Wednesday and Thursday. I could tell each day she was getting weaker and weaker. Friday, she answered the phone, but did not understand the conversation. "I will be leaving next Saturday to come see you," I told her. The last words she said to me were, "ok bye."

Because of work, I planned to leave Saturday, but I could not wait another day to go see Mama, after getting a call from Sarah on Monday morning, telling me that her condition had gotten worse. I told my boss I had to leave work immediately and go to Massachusetts to see about my mama. I had to hurry. I knew she was almost to the end. I stopped to pick up Tommy from the apartment he and Mama had shared. The ride to Massachusetts seemed long. There was silence between Tommy and myself. After arriving in Massachusetts, I went directly to Sarah's house to let her know I needed her to show me how to get to the hospital. She spent the day with Mama and was very tired, but she knew I had to get to the hospital quickly. As strong as I pretended I was, I needed Sarah and Tommy to give me strength. We went to the hospital together.

As I sat at Mama's bedside, I watched her motionless body. This was my friend, the only person who really knew the pain and suffering we had been through together. I was prepared to stay with her for as long as there was still breath in her body, not thinking about where I would lay my head. I had to stay with her during the night. Sarah had been with Mama all day and she wanted to go home, so she left and took Tommy with her. The late night drew near.

I wanted Mama to talk to me so badly, as I had wanted her to talk to me many times before. Only if she would open her eyes one more time and talk to me. I wanted Mama to know I was sorry for any meanness. There became a time, as a teenager, when I did not want to help with the younger children. I was tired of taking care of children. Even though I said some mean things at the time, I said them out of hurt. I was hurt because we did not have enough food and clothes already, and with two more children it was worse. It was more for me to have to worry about.

As the time passed, I noticed a loveseat against the wall in her room I could lay on to try to get some sleep. I stretched on the loveseat, I could not sleep. My mind kept thinking about our life throughout the years. I thought about the confusion and anger I once harbored. The anger was not necessarily against any individual, but against the situation of our lives, now all that anger turned into pity. I was determined to break the welfare chain that had been our life for so many years and I had succeeded. I was able to help Mama a little throughout the years. I never had much, but whatever I had, I made sure she had. I wished Mama's life could have been different. No matter how hard her life was, she still had dreams. Even when she was diagnosed with cancer, she had dreams.

I could tell, with each passing hour, Mama's condition got worse. She began to cough, and with each cough, her voice got weaker and weaker. I began to cough, too. Mama and I always had a coughing spell at the same time and she used to kid me about it. Mama and I had chronic coughs for years. I told her I inherited her cough. That night was no different. We coughed at the same time throughout the night, and I knew she wanted to say something, like she had for such a long time.

I got up to check on her and to wet her mouth with a small sponge. Her lips were so dry, and they had turned grey. I knew she was slipping away from me slowly. The nurse came into the room to change her bedding. Mama knew enough to hold on to the bed railing as the nurse turned her from side to side, but she never opened her eyes.

I had a lot of time to lie on the couch and think about our lives, wondering as the song goes "how we got over." The night was very long. It seemed to me the clock stood still. I could not sleep, as I continued to think about the past. I never wanted to go back to the past, because of the hard times as a child. I never had time to be a child. At five years old, I was tossed into a role no five-year-old should be in, not having the chance to be a kid, no time to think as a child. I was never anyone's baby, never cuddled. I never received the affection I needed. I was pushed into adult responsibility much too young; it seemed, at one time in my life, I never developed as a whole person. Confused as to why I was never happy as an adult, having situations not changing year after year eventually turned to anger. But, as maturity set in, anger turned to pity. We are all human and I know Mama loved me and I could not blame her for the life I've lived. I long ago stopped blaming anyone else for my downfall in my life. Her pain must have been just as great, if not greater than mine. I was very sad because Mama never found the happiness she deserved.

My only concern growing up was to take care of my mama and help her raise her children. I knew many times as a teenager I would say mean things especially after she had the last two girls. I told her I was not going to help her with her children anymore, but that was only in words. I continued to work after school to make sure my family had food to eat. I was very angry when Mama had more children. It had been the five of us and I did not want to have to take care of any more children.

I never told Mama how much I loved her. It's said actions speak louder than words. She knew by my actions I loved her and the rest of the family. I did all I knew how to make their lives easier, but she needed me to say the words "I Love You," and it was hard to say. I needed to hear those words from her. Mama was never affectionate toward her children and we grew up the same way, not being able to express our feelings toward each other. All my brothers and sisters loved Mama dearly and she loved all of us, we just did not know how to say it. It would have been so different if we had grown up showing our affection with hugs or kisses. I never remember getting a kiss from Mama, until I became an adult. She became more affectionate as she grew older. Mama's love for her children was never doubted, even if we did not get hugs and kisses. She was always home. She never left us alone. She could not provide us with material things, but she was there. She never went out in bars, nor did she drink alcohol. She was content when she was at home, not necessarily happy, but content. Her grandchildren made her smile through her sadness.

I continued to go to Mama's bedside to let her know I was still there and I would not leave. I wanted so much to kiss her cheeks, but I felt hypocritical kissing her now that she was dying, and I hadn't kissed her earlier. I did not want my children to grow up like I did, so I learned to be affectionate with them, even as they grew older, but I never learned to express my feeling toward Mama and my siblings.

I wish I had told Mama, in words, how much I loved her. She knew by my actions I loved her and the rest of the family, because I did all I knew how to make their lives easier. As a child, I knew I would do better for myself one day. No one told me I had to break the welfare chain, I knew in my heart I had to be the one to do it. I never made much money, but I always had a job. I was able to help Mama a little throughout the years. I could see what being on welfare did for us as a family. Sure, we got a check on the first of each month, but it was never enough. If Mama had good health during her younger years, I knew she would have rather worked than have her children on welfare, but she was not able to, and welfare was the only way for us to survive.

I felt good when I did something for my mama. As an adult I made sure she had food to eat, if I was aware of her needs. Many times, when I visited Mama, she would not tell me she did not have food for my sisters and brothers. The only way I knew she was out of food was when I opened her refrigerator and there was nothing in it. I could not do for them as much as I did when I was younger. I had a family of my own I was raising. I had gotten married right out of high school and had three children by the time I was twenty-one years old. I just could not help as much as I wanted to, but I did my best.

I had to stop thinking about the past and get some sleep. I was in the habit of repeating the twenty-third Psalm from the Bible when I could not fall asleep at night, which would always work for me, therefore I began to repeat:

The Lord is my Shepherd; I shall not want.
He maketh me to lie down in green pastures:
He leadeth me beside the still waters.
He restoreth my soul:
He leadeth me in the paths of righteousness for His name' sake.

Yea, though I walk through the valley of the shadow of death,
I will fear no evil: For thou art with me;
Thy rod and thy staff, they comfort me.
Thou preparest a table before me in the presence of mine enemies;
Thou annointest my head with oil; My cup runneth over.

Surely goodness and mercy shall follow me all the days of my life,
and I will dwell in the House of the Lord forever. Psalm 23

I finally fell asleep for a short time and daylight beamed through the windows of the hospital room, as I opened my eyes. I was confused as to where I was and then I realized I was in the hospital with Mama. I immediately jumped to my feet and went to her bedside. She was still breathing, but the sound of her breathing was very loud and different. She had made it through the night but I was afraid because I knew her time was not long. I called Sarah to tell her to get the family and come to the hospital right away. Two of my sisters had made it to Massachusetts from New York. My two sisters and two of my brothers came to the hospital with Sarah. There were six of us with Mama that morning. My brothers were not good at handling Mama's sickness

All morning long, we sat in her room talking and watching her. She had gone into a full coma, but I knew she was aware we were there. Aunt Gloria's daughter, my cousin, sent a minister from her church to come and pray with us. The minister's presence and prayers made us feel a little better. I asked the minister if he believed my mama had made her peace with God and that she was going to heaven. He replied that he believed she was tired and ready to leave this world, but he believed she was worried about all of her children. After the minister left, my two brothers decided to go for a walk, leaving me and my three sisters in the hospital room with Mama. I kept thinking about what the minister said, about her wanting to leave this world, but was worried about us. I wanted to assure her we would be fine.

I went to Mama's bedside. I kneeled down to talk to her in her ear. I sang "Precious Lord Take My Hands" before I began to talk to her. I told her it was all right for her to leave us, and that we would be okay. I told her that she had sisters and brothers who passed on and they were on the other side waiting for her. I told her she would be with her mother and father. I repeated to her, "Go on, Mama, I will take care of everyone," as the tears fell from my eyes. I knew she was worried the most about Tommy and I assured her he would be all right. It was about 1:45 in the afternoon when I finished talking to Mama. My three sisters sat in silence. I proceeded to go back to sit down, and began to write her obituary. As I wrote, my sisters stared at Mama. Sarah knew she was taking her last breath, because of her medical training. I stop writing to look toward Mama as she opened up her eyes and took one last breath at two o'clock in the afternoon. There was silence in the room for a moment. "She is gone!" Sarah exclaimed. No one cried at that moment, we just sat and stared at her. Finally, I went into the hallway of the hospital to find a nurse. The nurse came into the room to check her pulse, and said to us, "yes, she is gone."

Knowing it was a good thing my brothers left the hospital before Mama died, because it would have been very hard on all of us if they were there when she passed away, they would have never understood the peace and calmness in the room when she passed away. I believed God planned for my brothers not to be there for the final moment. They would not have been able to accept her death.

The six months the doctor predicted came so quickly. We were not prepared. I never gave up hoping for a miracle, because I do believe in miracles, but it was not to be for her to have a longer life. It was hard losing Mama, and planning for her funeral was not easy. I wanted so much to take her back to Upstate New York for her burial, but for financial reason, was unable. She died on March 30, 1993, and her funeral was April 3, 1993. Even thought I could not take her home to for burial, many of her friends and neighbors came to Massachusetts to pay their last respects. The outpouring of love by her friends and neighbors from her hometown was overwhelming.

No one knew the history of my family. It was something we never talked about, how we got to New York, and lived in the migrant labor camp. I erased that part of my life many years ago, but now I wanted to remember. I never wanted to relive that chapter in my life. We were not trying to escape the South with the second great migration of black folks to the North; it was just we had a chance to leave Alabama for four months and supposedly returned back home. Without knowing it, we became a part of the second great migration of black folks to the North, my mother and her five little children. An era ended when Mama passed. Life goes on even when the pain remains.

CHAPTER 9

WHERE ARE THEY NOW?

Papa

We never saw Papa after he left for Pittsburgh, Pennsylvania. We never heard from him again, except the ad in the Pittsburgh Courier newspaper, "looking for wife and four children." Mama heard through family members that he remarried, returned to Alabama and had more children. Mama's marriage to Papa was a mistake. He had been marry before and had older children. I do not think she knew what kind of man he was before she married him when she was only twenty years old.

Through Mama's oldest sister, who was married to Papa's uncle, she knew about Papa and his life after us. Papa didn't have a good life. His new marriage ended. One day, Mama got a letter from her sister reporting Papa killed a woman. He choked her to death. He went to prison for many years.

My brothers and sister never communicated with their father while he was in prison. They were grown and some had families of their own. After he was released from prison, he went back to the same life. Even though he was getting old, he loved younger women. He was not out of prison long before he killed another woman, one much younger than he was. This time he shot her nine times. Papa was sent back to prison, this time for life. The four children he and Mama had together never knew him as a father.

When Papa left Alabama going to Pittsburgh, they were young. Perhaps my three brothers remembered him, but my sister was much too young to remember. He never did anything for them while they were growing up. I am the one who had to go to work to help take care of them.

I was relieved Mama decided to travel to New York, rather than waiting for Papa to come back to Alabama. Things happen in mysterious ways. Mama could have been one of his victims. Somewhere down the line he became a violent man.

Papa died of cancer in prison while serving his life sentence for killing the second woman. He had died years earlier in my mind, when he excluded me as one of his children. My sister Diann and two of my brothers, Tyrone and Tommy, attended Papa's funeral. They were saddened to see him, but no tears were shed. Only his children were present at his funeral.

My brother Tyrone, who was four years old when Papa left, wanted to say a few words at the funeral. He said, as he stared at his father, "I do not know this man, but I do know that his blood runs through my veins." I imagine he died a lonely man.

Jake

After Jake left New York, he went back home to Mississippi and spent most of his time between Mississippi and Alabama, where he had relatives. Jake's carefree living finally got the best of him. He had a stroke and was never the same. He could not take care of himself. Jake was bound to a wheelchair and could not walk anymore. He was put into a nursing home by his family in Mississippi. Jake's children, my two sister and baby brother, did communicate with Jake, while he was in a nursing home. He had a good memory and was able to talk after his stroke.

His children wanted him closer to them, so they moved him from the nursing home in Mississippi to a nursing home in Atlanta. Sarah visited him regularly, so regularly she decided to bring him home with her. While Jake was with Sarah, I visited him. Even though I had not seen him for many years, he still remembered me. Sarah did not keep Jake for long in her home, it became too much for her to care for him, and therefore she put in back into a nursing home.

Jake died in a nursing home in Atlanta from the complication of a stroke. His funeral was small, with only family members. People who loved him in spite of how he lived surrounded him. He had grandchildren who got to know him before he passed away.

I wanted to give Jake one last honor; therefore, I sang a song at his funeral. I remembered when we were children Jake loved to sing and he sang gospel songs to us. He had a wonderful voice. His body was taken back to his home in Mississippi for burial.

Tommy

My beloved brother Tommy suffered throughout his life with his illness. It progressed, as he got older. He was not able to work to take care of himself, though he tried very hard to work. Along with his colostomy, his spine was twisted; he had pancreas disease and kidney problems. He never gave up hope – hope for a better life. He had big dreams, just like Mama. Never to my knowledge did Tommy feel his condition was a hindrance to his life. After all, it was the only life he knew. Being the oldest, as a young girl, I lived with his handicap as if it was my handicap. The family never thought of him as abnormal. He never considered himself abnormal. He was born with his condition, a colostomy. Many people are forced to get a colostomy later in life after living a normal life, but Tommy never knew a normal life as others did, because of his birth defect.

Tommy left New York and moved to Georgia, where he became ill. His colostomy had deteriorated to the extent that there were not enough large intestines to perform surgery to correct his illness. After more than twenty surgeries, he had no more large intestines left to cut. During each operation, a portion of his large intestine had been cut off. Therefore, his small intestine had to be used. A surgical procedure called an ileostomy was performed, which was the only thing that could help him. The doctors at a major hospital in the area he lived in performed his ileostomy. He did not have any medical insurance, but the hospital did not deny him service. His surgery was not without complications. He told me how much pain he was had after the surgery. He accepted his pains and kept going.

I visited him every day in the hospital. He depended on me to communicate with his doctors. I had been going to the hospital to see him since he was a little boy. Every time he became sick, he stayed in the hospital for one to two weeks. It was not unusual for him to call me when he became hospitalized. He called from the hospital to update me on his condition and I would rush to the hospital to be with him, and to make sure he had what he needed.

Tommy applied for Disability Social Security benefits for many years, but Social Security always denied him. They said he was able to work. His health deteriorated with each passing day. He tried to work. He would do odd jobs, but no one hired him permanently since he didn't have an education or job skills. There were times he was homeless and slept under the bridge, not because he had to, but because he was very independent and did not want to be a burden on the rest of the family. He wanted to live on his own. After Mama passed, I knew he felt alone at times. I think he appreciated me more as we became older.

One June morning, my sister Sarah in Atlanta told me Tommy had gone to the hospital by ambulance with severe stomach pains. The emergency department was waiting for a room to become available to admit him into the hospital. I did not think much about him going to the hospital, because of his history of illness. I told myself I would wait until he was assigned a room, and then I would call to talk to him. In the past whenever Tommy was in the hospital, he always assured me he was going to be all right. I expected him to tell me the same thing when I called after a room was assigned. I did not know how serious his illness was this time. If I had known, I would have rushed to him.

Tommy passed away before I could talk to him. It will always hurt because I did not talk to him before he died. He was my baby from the day he was born. Even when I was five years old, he was my baby. To have him die without saying good-bye will always be with me. I hope he knew how much he meant to me. Tommy was only fifty-six years old when he died. He truly suffered his lifetime, with the many surgeries he had, there was no place on his stomach for the doctors to cut anymore. Tommy's cause of death was not from his lifelong illness, but I knew his body was just worn out. He went into cardiac arrest, something much unexpected.

Tommy was a true survivor against all odds. He remained positive and believed he could do anything. He had a talent for repairing old televisions and radios as a young man, his fingers were magical.

Tommy's funeral was Thursday, June 5, 2008. The day of his funeral, a letter from Social Security arrived for him, it was a denial letter. I was very angry when I saw the denial letter. My brother died and they said he was able to work. In other words, they were saying he was not sick enough to receive benefits. He had no work history, but the agency wanted a work history from him. He had lived in the back of a store, working for the storeowner to earn enough money to live. In fact, the owner called the ambulance to take Tommy to the hospital.

If I could get a letter to TJ since I did not get to see him before he left this world, this is what it would say:

Dear "TJ," as friends and family so fondly called you. You slipped into God's arms before I could say goodbye. Amidst all your suffering, you were always strong, never complaining. Did you know you were my hero? Your strength through the years was my strength. Your energy was my energy. You will always be in my heart and thoughts. My only consolation is I know you are in a better place. Only if I had been financially able to make your life easier, I would have done that for you. I will truly miss you. If I could wish you back to this earth, it would only be if things were different for you — a life without pain and sorrow, a life without any handicap, and a life of normalcy as the world sees it.

I had always been there for you and it hurt me that you left me and I did not get a chance to be there for you for the last time, as I had in the past. Your last hours were without family. You died alone and that hurts when I think about it. The only thing that makes me feel better is to know Jesus was with you. Your brothers and sisters were coming to see you TJ, only if you could have waited for us to get there. If I had known how sick you were, I would have been beside you to hold your hand, and to pray with you, only if I had known!

One day we will all meet again and rejoice together in our glorified bodies. I can truly say your spirit is with me every day. Rest in peace, my brother. Love, your big sister (Gull)

My other brothers and sisters

All my brothers and sister moved from up North to Georgia except the one in California. Without Mama, it was easy to leave. We had nothing up North anymore. When the opportunity arrived for my husband and me to leave New York, my siblings wanted to leave, too. The change was good for the family; we all looked forward to a new start.

Diann lives in Atlanta, after leaving Buffalo, New York. She has a job working for a major finance company. She has two adult children, a son and a daughter, Mama did get to see her two children before she died. The move to Georgia has been rewarding for Diann.

Thomas lives in California. He is self-employed and has a talent for carpentry. Life has been difficult in California for him, but he has managed to overcome some obstacles that were in his path. He has two children, a son and daughter. Mama did see his children before she died.

Tyrone lives in Atlanta, with his wife. He relocated to Georgia from Massachusetts. Life has not been easy since he left Massachusetts. Without the proper education, it has been hard for him. He likes living in the South. Even though he was only four years old when we left Alabama, he remembers a little about our life. As told to me by Tyrone, his words were, "Life as hard in Alabama, but at least we did have a little food to eat. In New York, there were many times there was no food. After all is said and done, we never hurt or killed anybody, never were in jail for anything serious." He has a daughter who was eight years old when Mama died. She spent a lot of time with her grandma.

Sarah moved to Georgia from Massachusetts about the same time I left New York in 1994. She lives in Atlanta with her adult children and grandchildren. Life has been hard for her in Georgia but she loves the South. To her home is where the heart is.

Jean is the youngest daughter of the family. She left Yonkers, New York to relocate to Atlanta. She has many talents and lives a successful life in Georgia. She has no children.

Rod is the baby son of the family. He left Massachusetts to relocate to Atlanta. The change was especially good for him because Mama's death was very hard on him. He has done well for himself. The family is proud of him.

CHAPTER 10

CONCLUSION

LEAVING ALABAMA AS A child and moving to Upstate New York was not the life I expected, but it was the life I was destined to live. I often wonder what life would have been like if we never arrived in New York on the bean bus. What would we have done differently in Alabama than what was done in New York? The whole purpose of the trip was to survive and strive for a better life. My three sisters, three brothers, and I continued to accept the challenges of life. It wasn't the same without Mama and Tommy.

I could see what I had known from an early age – education was the key for a successful life. I worked most of my life but never got to where I wanted to be. I realized during time the importance of a college degree. A high school diploma was great to have in my younger years, but a college education is necessary. I looked to the next generation for major improvement, and it happened. We as a family are not where I wanted us to be, but there was victory in the younger generation, "our children." With good educations and college degrees, our children made a difference and changed the course of our family tree. None of Mama's children attended college; we were too busy with day-to-day work making a living for our families. Mama would be proud of her grandchildren's accomplishment.

I do not know what happened to other migrant families who travelled to Upstate New York from the South to do seasonal work, but one season for my family changed our lives forever, not so much for the good. With all the other migrant families who returned to the South, my hope would be that those families stayed strong and each generation was better off than the previous. I am sure some of them did stay strong, even if it had to be the next generations.

The hardship I experienced as a child not only made me strong physically and mentally, but also spiritually. I never turned to drugs, tobacco or alcohol for comfort. I felt good knowing I did all I could for my Mama, brothers and sisters at an early age, and that is what had helped me to not give up. We did not ask to be born poor, and I thank God for the test he put me through in this life, a test of survival. Only the strong will survive and survive I did, not as good as I would have liked, but good enough to make me appreciative and a better person. My younger years in Upstate New York, I gained what I needed to be the person I am today, a person of hard work and integrity. My children followed in my footsteps, hopefully my grandchildren will also.

Every mistake I made in life I learned something from. Some mistakes I could fix and some I could not. Life is full of problems we have no control over without bringing problems on ourselves. I always tried to do the right thing and believed everyone should do the same. I was true to myself. As a young girl I promised myself that as an adult, I would not have my children on welfare, as we were as children. Because of my work habits which I formed at an early age and with the blessing of always having a job I kept that promise.

When I was fourteen years old, I met one of the women who served on that committee. She needed someone to clean her home, and I accepted the job. She became a second mother to me. She was my friend, a person I loved dearly; she inspired me throughout my younger years as well as into adulthood.

Even as a child, I was negative. Being confused about my surrounding and my family's situation, I distanced myself from disappointment by being negative. If I felt positive and something negative happened hurt would come. I learned to be negative about everything in my life. That way if something positive happened that was an unexpected plus in my life. I later realized negative thinking was just a way for Satan to bring and keep me down. It took me many years to realize negative thinking brings about negative results.

My friend Kathy taught me the values that were within me. She taught me to love myself and to be happy with whom I was, also to have a positive attitude and to know I am somebody. She made me believe in myself. She made me feel worthy with praises, praises I never got from Mama.

Many people have never heard about the migrant workers in Upstate New York, their living condition on the camps, and the back breaking hard work picking snap beans, a form of modern-day slavery nearly a century after the Civil War. Only the people in the areas where the camps were located knew about the living conditions the migrant workers endured, and only a few were still alive by 2012. Some of the people in the area formed a migrant committee in the 1950s. They soon realized the migrant workers were human beings, and helped by supplying blankets and other services. By the time my family arrived in the migrant labor camp in 1959, the living conditions had vastly improved compared to the early 1950s. The wages for a bushel of beans picked went from 30 cents a bushel to 50 cents. The camps made clean drinking water available to the workers. The camps began to fade the middle part of the 1960s, when not many workers came anymore.

There is little history known about the African-American seasonal migrant workers who came to Upstate New York to pick snap beans during the 1950s and early 1960s in the six camps. The African-American migrant workers in the North are a part of history that is not widely talked about; history I will never forget.

www.ingramcontent.com/pod-product-compliance
Lightning Source LLC
Chambersburg PA
CBHW022107050726
47591CB00002B/701